Station Master's Reflections

Station Master's Reflections

Images of railway life, 1954-64

David Holmes

BCA

LONDON   NEW YORK   SYDNEY   TORONTO

This edition published 1993 by BCA by arrangement with
Silver Link Publishing Ltd

CN 9810

Maps drawn by Christina Siviter

Printed and bound in Great Britain by Butler & Tanner Ltd,
Frome, Somerset

Contents

4-4-2T Nos 67398 and 67376, Peterborough North, 4.1 pm, 11.6.57

A busy station like Peterborough North would normally have two or three pilot locos in the days of steam. The two illustrated are carrying out the normal duties of such locos. No 67376 is approaching the up platform with empty stock - No 67398, on the left, is attaching a parcels van to the rear of a northbound train. With the quick reactions of youth (well, it was a long time ago!) I was able to catch the second loco in note the target number in the middle of the buffer beam. the split second between the post and the first loco.

Introduction

This book is an attempt to portray the railways of part of Britain during the period 1954 to 1964. It is seen through the eyes of a railwayman who was, and still is, a railway enthusiast. To a certain extent it is also a look from a different angle, that seen by a clerk and station master in the days of steam. During the period under review there were, of course, vast changes. In 1954 the old, pre-nationalisation railway still existed and provided an indispensible transport system. Most people didn't have cars in those days and road haulage was still in its infancy. The railways came in for a lot of criticism then but they continued to move the nation's passengers and freight as they had done for over 100 years.

This is a look at how the railways appeared to an interested observer during a ten-year period towards the end of steam. I have chosen 1964 as the closing date because, although there were still four years to go until the final sad day in 1968 when steam came to an end in this country, those years were rather depressing to one who had been privileged to see so much in the days when it seemed that steam would never end. I appreciate that many people found much of interest in the mid-1960s and thought themselves lucky to catch the last few years, but I will stick with my memories of a glorious time and the photos I was lucky enough to take.

The emphasis of the book is on freight. Nowadays more and more enthusiasts are turning to freight as passenger trains become more stereotyped, with so much emphasis on multiple units. Freight is the one area where there is still variety of livery and a continuation of loco haulage. But this book looks back to an era, not so long ago, when freight was even more varied, but not so well known. I took my share of photos of passenger trains, but what about this hidden side of the railway in the 1950s and early '60s?

Most people were completely unaware of the huge goods depots such as Leeds Hunslet Lane. This was a frightening place to a young clerk. Hundreds of people were employed at such depots and, as late as 1967, a 19th-century scene was evident. Wagons were pulled into the large warehouse by capstans, traversers moved the unloaded wagons across to the outgoing line where pilots waited outside to remove them and propel more loaded ones inside. Two-man gangs unloaded the sundries and took them around the warehouse to waiting trailers or wagons. All this has now gone, as have the coal drops, surely a North Eastern or Lancashire & Yorkshire speciality.

I well remember seeing a photo of a lovely SE&CR Wainwright 4-4-0 pulling a train of decrepit four-wheel passenger stock. The caption highlighted the difference between the loco and the coaches. In some ways the same applies to the freight scene. We've all seen photos of steam locos making lots of smoke and pulling the ubiquitous rakes of wagons, but how often do we hear about what was *in* the wagons? Still less have we thought about the people involved in loading, unloading and selling the down-to-earth freight which made so many railways profitable for many years. Even now it is Trainload Freight which makes one of the largest contributions to BR's wellbeing.

As a Goods Office clerk and Station Master, I was in an ideal position to observe the passing scene and record it on film during those last ten years of change when there was so much of interest to see. What was the railway trying to achieve during that period? Was it merely carrying on with the old ways and with a captive market, or was it, in the form of the Reshaping Plan of 1955, trying to make a fresh start? At the time I didn't know and, looking back, it would seem that the real steps towards a modern freight system were still some way off. At the time we just did our jobs and tried to provide a service for our customers.

Maybe it is sufficient, for the time being, to have a look at the period and form our own judgments. I have tried to provide comprehensive captions for the photographs in an attempt to highlight the less obvious items which were, nevertheless, part of the pervading interest of the railways. The chapters follow my career and I have tried to demonstrate what went on day to day, with a few comments on what I did personally. I hope it will prove to be of interest in throwing light on areas of a railway system in which we all find continuing fascination and, indeed, a way of life.

Acknowledgements

I would like to thank the following friends and colleagues, whose books proved to be very useful sources of reference: C.T. Goode, *The Railways of Leeds and Bradford*, and Roy Waring, *The Leeds New Line*. R. A. Cooke gave invaluable assistance with the maps.

'M7' 0-4-4T No 30131, Yeovil Town, 10.38 am, 2.7.60, 10.50 am (SO) to Yeovil Junction
The lovely branches of Devon and Somerset were well known, 30 years ago, for their charming little trains busily connecting equally attractive towns with the main line. Push-and-pull trains were very common, of course, and were ideal for the purpose. Slightly longer and busier branches, such as that to Exmouth, needed more substantial stock. Yeovil was a fascinating town with a surprisingly complex rail system; a glance at a pre-Grouping map will illustrate this. Suffice to say, nowadays passengers must take a taxi or a bus (shown in the BR timetable) to the Junction. Yeovil Town station and loco shed have now been replaced by a supermarket.

1

Rothwell, GN

August to October 1954

In 1954 the railway was still recovering from the war and strenuous efforts were being made to restore fast main-line passenger services. I well remember when the 'Queen of Scots' Pullman started running, and I used to see it often at Headingley going north. An hour or so later it would reappear heading south. How could it turn around so quickly? At that early age I didn't realise that there were two sets of stock! Later in the book I have included a section on Pullmans, as they were always of interest as well as being very photogenic.

Away from the main lines, however, there were many backwaters, and none was stranger or more suspended in time than the East & West Yorkshire Union Railway. For a short period 40 years previously there had been a passenger service, but it was not a success; the station buildings remained, however, at Robin Hood and Rothwell. The line ran across from one main line to another. It left the Leeds-King's Cross line, now electrified, at Lofthouse; at the Midland end there were pure pre-Grouping exchange sidings between the E&W Yorks and the Midland.

The other main features, and the reasons for the line's continued existence, were Lofthouse and Newmarket Collieries and the Robin Hood Coke Works; these have all now disappeared. Robin Hood may seem an odd name for a place many miles from Sherwood Forest, but it perpetuates Yorkshire's claim to be the home of the famous outlaw.

Rothwell and its three staff really had no reason to exist, even in 1954. The small goods yard received one or two wagons of coal each day from collieries just a few miles away. There was a Goods Agent, porter and junior clerk with, perhaps, five hours work a day between them.

There was also another person, a probationer clerk. It was the practice for many years for a new member of staff, on joining BR, to spend six months on probation to see if he was suitable for permanent employment. It really was inevitable that I would join the railways. At the age of five I had started collecting engine numbers when the first *ABC of LNER Locomotives* was published. At school, in Leeds, spotting was the craze. It kept us out of mischief - usually - and broadened our horizons. What other schoolboy would be keen to visit exotic places like Crewe and Doncaster? The only question was - in what capacity would I join? An interview and medical at York, a reference from my headmaster and a few GCEs were all that were needed.

At about that time the railways were beginning to feel the first effects of road competition and I well remember attending one of my first Stephenson Locomotive Society meetings in Leeds. Dr W. A. Tuplin, the famous railway writer and commentator, was our Chairman. Each year he delighted us with a lecture but, on this occasion, he was late. Eventually he burst through the door and collapsed into a chair.

'I've just travelled from Huddersfield in the worst form of transport devised by man,' he gasped, 'and to make matters worse I had to drive the damned thing myself!'

I don't suppose the railway service was much better at the time, but there have been great improvements in recent years.

It was still the policy for almost every station or depot to have its own manager, no matter how small the traffic and, consequently, the grade of job. There was also still a division between goods, passenger and operating duties. This meant that the Goods Agent looked after goods commercial aspects, visiting customers, etc, whilst the Station Master at Robin Hood covered the operating duties, safety of the line and similar matters. We shall see more of this later in the book. Suffice to say that neither man had a great deal to do; nor had the porter, whose main job was to keep the place clean and collect the few wagon labels from the incoming coal trucks.

At all goods depots, including thousands of small yards attached to passenger stations, there were certain practices in common. Received traffic was meticulously recorded by a checker or porter, and the details, including one wagon label, were brought to the office for the clerk to record in the received book. When the goods were unloaded, the other label would be removed and the clerk again informed so that he could calculate any demurrage (detention) charges necessary - this occurred if the free period had been exceeded. The customer was sent an advice each day when there were new arrivals and informed that he had the 'day of receipt of advice plus the following day' in which to unload the wagons. Other charges would be for fixed space, if, for example, a customer rented an area of so many square yards, perhaps to stack coal. On a secret day each month excess space occupied by each coal merchant was measured - the date was kept secret so that the merchants could not rush round clearing up to avoid the excess charge! Large tape measures were supplied for this purpose, but if they were lost, or if only one person was available to do the job, it was quite common for him to just stride it out to obtain a very rough and ready measurement.

An invoice was received for inwards traffic and many thousands of these were passed around the country each day in large, appropriately marked envelopes - this despite the so-called 'abolition of invoicing' that had taken place a few years previously. The abolition had meant a vast reduction in work as, before that, every single sundries item had been invoiced, creating work for thousands of clerks who produced them and checked them off at the receiving end. There was no forwarded traffic at Rothwell but we shall see later what this entailed elsewhere.

The regular locos on the line were the ancient Great Northern 'J52' saddle tanks. One of these, usually 68868 or 68875, worked two trips from Robin Hood to Stourton each day, and on the midday trip would return propelling the odd wagon to Rothwell before running round it and placing it in the yard. This trip also took away a small wooden box containing 'Hollerith' cards to go to Mineral Accounts in Peterborough. This came about in the following manner: because the junior clerk had so little to do it was decided that at Rothwell, as at several similar places, some extra work would be found rather than withdraw the post. Coal waybills were just the thing!

Two or three collieries could send their forwarded consignment notes to a local station and the clerk could copy all the details onto waybills in triplicate - one copy was for the destination, one was to be retained and the third copy was a card about 7 inches by 3 inches. The latter were packed in a suitably constructed box along with the consignment notes and sent to Peterborough for charging. If the destination did not receive an invoice they would write to you requesting one. Owing to the fact that invoice = consignment note = charging, you had a reasonably foolproof revenue protection system which served the railways for over a hundred years. Needless to say it was extremely labour intensive and consignment through TOPS (the computerised Total Operations Processing Systems) in due course completely replaced it.

Three months of this, together with intensive study of goods station work and accounts, insisted upon by the junior clerk, no less, was my introduction to BR at the early age of 16, but it was a suitable beginning and a good introduction to a life largely unknown to the outside world despite the large number of people working on freight at the time.

'K1' 2-6-0 No 62051, Ardsley, 9.23 pm, 28.6.61, freight
At 9.23 pm this was the latest evening shot I ever took. 'K1s' were not very common in the area and this one's operations seem to be creating some interest amongst the yard staff. The various yards at Ardsley covered an immense acreage but all have now gone as have the mixture of vans making up the train. The main Leeds-Doncaster line is behind the engine and the line to Morley and Bradford is beyond.

'J39' 0-6-0 No 64919, Thackley, 6.50 pm, 13.7.61, 6.0 pm Keighley-Wrenthorpe Class H freight
This was the sort of little-known branch line where you needed access to the Working Timetable to have any hope of photographing a train. It was a GN line running parallel to the Midland for some distance but, whereas the latter kept to the bottom of the valley, this line climbed the hillside before turning right through the delightfully named Idle towards Laisterdyke. As in many other parts of the West Riding, this train could have travelled via a different route at one time, ie Queensbury. However, it would not then have been able to serve Shipley. The 'J39' is working hard up the gradient and is a long way from Sunderland, the name painted on the bufferbeam in LNER fashion, and its previous home shed.

'1F' 0-6-0T No 41797 and '4F' 0-6-0 No 44238, Stourton shed, 12.56 pm, 13.4.55
Despite the BR number and logo, we have here a very primitive class of loco on coaling duties. The half cab reminds you of the pictures of the earliest locos which had little more than a weatherboard in front of the driver - even in 1955 No 41797 did not offer much more. Maybe it didn't matter too much if she was just used within the precincts of the shed. Note the old-type coaling plant with the wagons being pushed up a sharp incline and unloaded by shovel.

'J52' 0-6-0ST No 68837 and 'J6' 0-6-0 No 64262, Rothwell, 9.50 am, 16.10.54, Mrs Cotton's excursion to Blackpool
Mrs Cotton was the wife of a former Station Master on the East & West Yorkshire Union Railway and in 1954 she and Mr Cotton were at Stanningley. However, the enterprising lady still organised a couple of excursions each year from Rothwell and Robin Hood for the benefit of the local people who took full advantage of the offer. These were the only passenger trains to be seen on the line; the 'J52' is one of the regular day-to-day locos which worked the freight trains. Only one platform was available at each station but this was sufficient. The Rothwell loop can be seen in the foreground and the line into the goods yard runs behind the train. Note the excursion number in front of the chimney, reference to which would be given in the Special Traffic Notice showing the timing details. A homburg-hatted official peers out from the cab of the 'J6' but makes no remark to the solitary photographer.

'J52' 0-6-0ST No 68875, Robin Hood, 6.55 pm, 24.5.60
This is the line where I started my railway career. The 'J52' Class of GN saddle tanks worked nearly all the trains on this line including the Newmarket Colliery branch. Later, Austerity 'J94' tanks took over before the line disappeared for ever many years ago. Note the engineers' trolley in the foreground - this would be wheeled along the short length of track at right angles to the main line before being manhandled on to the line to carry track repair materials. The remains of the old passenger station stood nearby, left over from the passenger service of 40 years previously - yet Robin Hood still had a Station Master in the 1960s. Robin Hood Coke Works supplied some of the traffic for the line in addition to Newmarket and Lofthouse collieries.

'5MT' 4-6-0 No 45207, Lofthouse, 8.0 pm, 24.5.60, Up Class D freight
Leeds to King's Cross electrics now run along this line and EMUs call at Outwood station which was recently built here to replace the long-closed station out of the picture to the right. In the background is Lofthouse Colliery. In common with most collieries which eventually closed, this has now completely disappeared, as has the line to Rothwell which went off to the left of the colliery buildings. A 'Black Five' was not a particularly common freight loco on this route, but the train is a fairly typical fitted freight of the period with most of the wagons reaching their destinations next morning. There are A and B type containers as well as the usual 'vanfits' and a brake van. Across the back of the picture runs the north-to-east side of the triangle, which lines went to Stanley and Castleford, with a second entrance to Newmarket Colliery adding to that from Robin Hood.

'4MT' 2-6-4T No 42324, Leeds Central, 11.54 am, 22.10.60, 11.55 am (SO) to Manchester Victoria
I took this photo to illustrate just how smoky some stations could be in steam days. Add to this the aroma from Soapy Watson's factory next door, and you could cut the air with a knife. Note the pipe in the right foreground for filling the water tanks in the coaches - no wonder notices warned 'Not drinking water'. Steam heating of the coaches is in use as it is after 1 October in accordance with the General Appendix to the Working Timetables. There is a set of LNER stock on the right and a general air of drabness about the place. It is amazing the difference that terrazzo floors have made to many stations now, but not here, unfortunately, as Central station closed in 1967.

'O4' 2-8-0 No 63570, Ardsley, 2.55 pm, 5.11.60, 2.45 pm (SO) Ardsley Old Coal Yard to York Class J freight
A footpath alongside the line is always a joy to the railway enthusiast, but this one was better than most. Not only did it run for a long way alongside the main Leeds-King's Cross line, but it also had yards with considerable activity on both sides. You could walk from Ardsley station to the shed along here. An extra item of luxury was the provision of gas lighting along the path. The Robinson 'O4' was going to York, rather unusual for this class. Note the '8F' making smoke in the distance - this was a class not often seen at Ardsley. There is also an early diesel shunter in the background.

'3MT' 2-6-2T No 40181, Walton (previously known as Sandal & Walton), 2.21 pm, 11.3.61, 2.6 pm (SO) Cudworth-Leeds City

A pleasant scene on the Midland main line. The Saturday local is just running in but hasn't many passengers. The normal two-coach set has had an extra coach added; as a result there is a guard's brake in the middle of the train. Although it is Saturday afternoon heavy freight continues on the Goods line. Nowadays this is no longer a through route and carries just a handful of freight trains. The passenger stations have gone, even once busy junctions like Cudworth. An odd feature of this station was the use of sleepers, placed end-on, to form the platform edge.

The station garden has been partially abandoned. I remember a local paper catching out an unfortunate member of staff at a station about to go over to Pay Train operation. 'I suppose the lovely gardens will be abandoned then?' 'No, of course not.' 'Well, there won't be anybody here to tend them, will there?' 'Er, well, I suppose not'.

On departing, the train will soon cross the GN Leeds-Doncaster line, with which there was once a connection. On this line a new station has opened recently; known as Sandal and Agbrigg, it replaces the old Sandal station which closed many years ago.

'2F' 0-6-0 No 58136, Stourton, 12 noon, 19.5.55

Very much a case of points and signals with large numbers of wagons in Stourton Up yard, to the left, and Stourton Down, between which ran the Midland main line. Note the double slip point layout in the foreground. On Beeching's map this was one of the thickest, blackest lines, denoting perhaps the busiest freight line in the country. Now there is very little to be seen apart from the 1960s Freightliner depot. The loco shed, on the extreme right, was almost entirely devoted to freight locos. The old '2F' and the Johnson 0-6-0 tank in the distance are pure Midland Railway. A new marshalling yard was actually started during the early 1960s' enthusiasm for such places, but construction was then stopped, leaving only a cutting under the main Leeds-Castleford road.

'Jubilee' 4-6-0 No 45615 *Malay States*, Woodlesford, 11.36 am, 18.3.61, 9.5 am excursion Leicester London Rd-Leeds City
It is nearly spring and the Engineers Department has been along here cutting down the abundant undergrowth to ensure that the drivers get a good view ahead. It always seems a pity to see this and also the effects of the weedkiller train on the lineside trees and bushes but it is, of course, necessary. This line is still in use with regular services between Leeds and Knottingley, Goole and Sheffield via Castleford. My lineside pass allowed me to be at this location near Woodlesford station, a pleasant spot with staggered platforms. There were several collieries hereabouts with charming steam shunting engines, but only a few slag heaps remain to remind us of earlier activities. In many cases even the slag heaps have been contoured and turned into grassy hills.

'J39' 0-6-0 No 64760, Beeston, 6.37 pm, 15.8.60, Up freight
A typical local trip of the period, but expensive to run - you needed driver, fireman and guard, of course, and had to find a brake van. Add to this the necessary lamps and other equipment and it was quite a major operation to move a few empty POWs - 16-ton coal trucks still known in some parts as Private Owner Wagons from the days when they belonged to the old colliery companies. The train is going to Wrenthorpe GN yard at Wakefield and continues the old system of pre-Grouping yards and 'trips'. This was soon to be overtaken by the opening of Healey Mills new yard which resulted in the closure of many of the smaller yards and the complete change in the system of trip working.

'L1' 2-6-4T No 67764, Drighlington & Adwalton, 2.59 pm, 14.7.62, Bradford portion of 10.50 am from King's Cross
There were mixed reports about the performance of these engines and they did not have a long life - most had gone by the following year. I always liked them, however, and associated their appearance with that of the 'A1s' and 'A2s' which were also built in the late 1940s. This was at a time when I was becoming very keen on railways.
   The junction of the two routes to Wakefield is indicated by the signals - to the left was the line via Ardsley, while the other dropped down to Batley and Ossett. The station actually had electric lighting, fairly rare at many places in the area. Note the metal waiting room sign on the door on the right.

2
Leeds Marsh Lane
November 1954 to May 1955

This was a good place to continue my career in the goods department. In Leeds there were three very large depots, Hunslet Lane, Hunslet East and Wellington Street, and a smaller depot at Whitehall Road; the latter was the only one to remain into the 1980s but has now closed. Suburban stations each had their own goods yards, including Marsh Lane.

A great deal went on here, albeit in a quiet sort of way. This was partly due to the fact that the offices were bombed during the war and the depot later became a satellite under Hunslet East. As a result there were only five clerks and a fairly small number of Conciliation staff.

Traffic, however, was considerable and varied. Starting at the passenger station, let us work our way across the depot. The original Leeds & Selby Railway started from Marsh Lane, and when the line was later extended to Leeds City station it was laid on a succession of bridges and embankments. Marsh Lane passenger station was, therefore, above street level. I used to go up the steps from the goods office at about 9.10 am most days to see the 'North Briton' running through behind an 'A2/2'. 'D49s' and 'D20s' worked the local services to Harrogate, York and Selby.

Next was the sack warehouse which held about ten thousand grain sacks at times and brought a wonderful aroma of the country into a rather depressing area of the city. There was a full-time sack clerk whose job it was to trace the movements of the sacks from initial hire to a farmer to eventual return from, probably, a bakery; the sacks might be hired at a country station and returned from somewhere else after passing through several merchants' responsibilities. Often these people did not even see them, but there was a free period for each transfer and they all had to be traced. To this day, if you listen to the 6.10 am Farming Programme on Radio 4 you will often hear from a Leeds grain merchant, one of the many dealt with by our sack clerk. The sack business was

all sold off in about 1964.

Next, across the low-level yard from the office and sack warehouse, was another very large warehouse with banana-ripening rooms in the basements; above was stored cement, grain, sugar and cattle food, quite a mixture but part of a nationwide business of storage and distribution carried on by BR. The traffic arrived, of course, by rail and was unloaded by BR staff. The junior clerk kept the stock records, with inwards and outwards movements being shown on appropriate stock sheets so that you and the customer knew what was on hand and when to send in more. An ancient lorry driver with an equally decrepit 3-ton cob-and-tank trailer dutifully called in at the office each time he took a load of barley out to Tetley's brewery - he would appear at the sliding windows smoking his pipe. The warehouse had, of course, a BR cat with appropriate milk ration, which was also faithfully recorded through the books.

Beyond the warehouse was the small fish dock and office. Generally four vans of fish arrived from Hull at about 5 am, and like everything else they were 'tripped' down from Neville Hill. Delivery sheets had to be compiled and phone calls answered. Sometimes a large box of fish could be seen moving by itself along the dock, and behind it a cheerful dwarf chap! Nearly all the fish arrived by rail in those days, so the local trade was understandably worried if there were any delays.

There was then an unusual feature, a private siding inside a covered shed inside the goods yard, and here were received such delights as Scottish jams and marmalade. Many were the claims and complaints about damage due to the containers conveyed on 'conflats' receiving rough shunts. Someone had to inspect the damage and authorise payment of claims. I do not remember receiving any cheap products as a result, but at many places BR staff did benefit by being able to purchase, for instance, battered and probably labelless cans of soup. Often you didn't know what you were getting until you opened the can!

There then followed two coal yards, each with its own weighbridge. The first was a coal-drop yard receiving hopper wagons for bottom door discharge. The office was down below the level of the line. The last yard was a flat coal yard where ordinary 16-ton wagons were unloaded by shovel into sacks on a flat lorry, a laborious and dirty job as well as involving heavy lifting of hundredweight bags and stooping through the side door of the wagon.

BR received considerable revenue for all these traffics. At the peak of the barley season, as many as 20 'vanfits' a day were received from East Anglia. The storage traffic involved carriage and storage charges; coal brought in weighing charges, fixed and excess space. Where BR carried out deliveries by road, further charges were involved. Pay was pretty low, about £7 a week for a porter and less than £5 for the junior clerk. The highest-paid man was the chap who was called out to feed and water cattle in transit. This

traffic was mainly from Holyhead and, if they were due for feeding when they arrived in the West Riding, Marsh Lane was the place.

The pilot was a 'J72' 0-6-0, usually No 68672, and this was kept busy shunting the various sidings. Altogether it was an interesting place, with pleasant people to work with. The sack clerk was an ex-RAF type with handlebar moustache - after 30 ops over Germany I could never understand how he could settle down to such a mundane task, but he seemed happy enough. The chief was an old stager from the pre-war days when the LNER would, perhaps, give you a day's notice before sending you off to lodge at a remote country station for the next few years. He was a cheerful type who helped me a great deal in my early days on BR and I was more than happy to go to the local shop for his daily packet of fags. A large coal fire heated a small part of the office, at least, and I spent many a happy lunch hour reading a book beside it in the cold winter weather.

'J72' 0-6-0T No 68672, Marsh Lane, 1.40 pm, 1.12.54
This loco was the regular pilot for many years and was, of course, a North Eastern Railway engine on duty at an NER location 30 years after the demise of that company. The rail weighbridge is on the left - I do not remember it being used, but its main purpose would be for such traffic as scrap metal which normally could not be weighed before being loaded into the wagon. In the right distance is the deep cutting on the way to Neville Hill. This was partly in tunnel at one time but was opened out at great expense many years ago.

Standard 2-6-4T No 80120, Headingley, 7.19 pm, 17.6.61, 2.55 pm King's Cross-Harrogate

The Headingley up starter glimpsed on the left has the Cardigan Road distant slotted underneath. I was always rather mystified by this as it was very nearly a mile to Cardigan Road, but it was down quite a steep gradient which explained the need for adequate warning of the situation; for example, if shunting was taking place at Cardigan Road a train passing Headingley needed plenty of warning so that speed could be reduced in time to stop. On the other hand it was too great a distance for a manual pull, so there must have been a motor. Most of the time, though, Cardigan Road was switched out so the distant fell with the home, making a great clatter and announcing the imminence of the next train.

Several Standard Class '4' tanks were drafted into this area to replace the 'Hunts' and 'D20s' on the Harrogate services. It was common, at the time, to have LNER stock on these trains. Nowadays there is still one train each way between King's Cross and Harrogate. There is a footpath under the trees on the right, and this was an ideal spot from which to watch trains and the shunting in the goods yard. The shunting neck can be seen, now overgrown.

'3MT' 2-6-2T No 40148, Engine Shed Junction, 12.20 pm, 24.6.61, 12.15 pm Leeds City-Cudworth

A busy scene outside Holbeck shed. The large-boilered Stanier Class '3' has the advantage of upper quadrant signals complete with a rather charming miniature repeater necessitated by the intervening bridge which restricted the driver's view. The early DMU has to make do with a colour light signal. The signal box is beyond the bridge and opposite the shed which survives to this day in a reduced form - gone are the old roundhouses and coaling plant. On the left a 'Jubilee' has just come out of the shed yard steamed up ready to back down to Leeds City station. On the right a disreputable fence completes the picture.

'J50' 0-6-0T No 68898, Holbeck High Level, 4.56 pm, 25.4.62, empty stock for Leeds Central
A bit of smart work by the signalman - he has already thrown the signals to danger after the passage of this train. 'J50s' were the normal engines on these workings for very many years; they were known as 'Submarines' by the local trainspotting fraternity. The only reason for this, as far as I know, was that there was a sloping end to the front of the side tanks. It was easy going down to Central but they had to work hard coming back. The stock has just emerged from Copley Hill carriage sidings which, like so many other such sidings, have now gone, but the lines swinging to the right still survive on the way to Bradford via Bramley. It is noticeable that even the empty stock for a local stopping train needed to be worked to and from the carriage sidings by a separate loco. By this date DMUs had taken over most of the local services.

Note the long trap in the right-hand line, which would help to keep an over-running train clear of the drop down the embankment. Such 'traps' (for forward movements) or 'catch points' (for backward) always seem rather crude, although effective. It is a question of the lesser of two evils if a train or wagons should get away in an uncontrolled or unauthorised movement. Most catch points have now gone - they tended to be on uphill gradients, but the loose-coupled unbraked wagons that they were intended to derail no longer exist.

'Jubilee' 4-6-0 No 45581 *Bihar and Orissa*, Whitehall Junction, 3.50 pm, 25.4.62, Leeds City-Manchester parcels
Whitehall Road goods yard is on the right of this picture, and *Bihar and Orissa* is on a then little-used connection on its way to Manchester. Later, when Leeds City was rebuilt, this became the main LNW route out of Leeds; indeed, further plans are now being made to re-arrange the layout and install new track in this area to alleviate congestion. The line going away to the left distance, approaching Leeds, used to be known as 'Patience Corner' because of the delays experienced there. While the enthusiast didn't mind sitting in a train amidst the activity, the general public were not amused. The Midland main line, on the left, is protected by a sand drag in case of a runaway on the line from Manchester. Note the footpath down below - this was one of the two rather forbidding entries to Holbeck Low Level station, and a Mecca for trainspotters.

There is some steam heating on the train for the benefit of the guard further back, who would otherwise require the provision of a stove van. The leading wagons convey fish and so do not need heating! This train continued to be worked by steam until the end of 1967, one of the last in the Leeds area.

'B1' 4-6-0 No 61237 *Geoffrey H. Kitson*, Marsh Lane, 10.20 am, 2.2.55, 10.17 am Leeds-York
A view of the east end of Marsh Lane station showing the huge warehouse in which large amounts of barley, cement, sugar and, in the cellars, bananas were stored. Next to the loco is the sack warehouse containing vast quantities of grain sacks awaiting the harvest season. Two types of hopper wagon can be seen on the right - one is an ancient NE wooden-bodied type, used for many years in that part of the country for local domestic coal as well as for discharge at the shipping staiths on the Tyne, Wearside and at Blyth. There is a bad steam leak between the engine and the first coach, depriving the passengers of most of the heat on a cold morning!

'D49' 4-4-0 No 62740 *The Bedale*, 5.29 pm, 5.8.57, Harrogate, 5.30 pm to Leeds via Arthington
A fine view with an NER ambiance showing a train nearly ready to depart. The clock shows a minute to go and the NER signal is lowered. Note the fairly substantial subsidiary signal underneath; at some places on the NER, for example Durham viaduct, the sub-signal would be off too. The banner signal on the right is also clear, indicating that the next home signal, out of sight, is showing a proceed aspect - these are still used even in modern multiple aspect signalling areas. The Inspector is blowing his whistle but the driver and fireman are relaxing on a platform bench - after all, there is still a minute left! This station has now been modernised and the platform on the extreme right has gone. Note the two-way trap points and interlocking in the line on the left.

'J27' 0-6-0 No 65827, Malton, 10.54 am, 16.4.58
A scene from history outside Malton shed. The old 'J27' has seen better days but was ready for anything during the winter just ended - a furled tarpaulin sits on the back of the cab for tender-first running. The old vans in the background present an incredible sight even in 1958, having been retained for tool van purposes. Note the length of the two-road shed, which reminds us that Malton was at the hub of quite a number of lines, to Driffield, Pilmoor, Whitby and Forge Valley, as well as being situated on the busy York-Scarborough route. The chequer sign on the shed wall indicates limited space between the wall and the line for pedestrians entering the shed.

'Patriot' 4-6-0 No 45538 *Giggleswick*, Kilburn High Road, 11.48 am, 7.7.60
Giggleswick was a regular loco on the Leeds-Morecambe run in the the 1940s along with *E. Tootal Broadhurst*, but now she is reduced to working empty stock into Euston, a type of job prevalent at the time. Nowadays most trains can turn round very quickly after a brief sweep out. Even before the advent of the DVTs (Driving Van Trailers), effectively turning a loco-hauled train into a double-ended multiple unit, there was less tendency to drag stock all the way out to Willesden in any great numbers. The slow line platforms such as those shown here have now gone except at Queens Park. Note the electric signal with the 'feather' indicating a left-hand turn-out beyond the rather forbidding High Road shop-backs above.

'A3' 4-6-2 No 60064 *Tagalie*, Northallerton, 12.57 pm, 4.2.61, Delavel-Welwyn Garden City vans
Tagalie was one of the earliest rebuilt 'A3s' to receive German smoke deflectors and I was lucky to catch her just before this happened. The train is one of the famous empty van trains from Tyneside (the other one ran to Manchester). The actual origins and destinations varied over the years, but both trains were always worth waiting for due to the variety of locos and double heading employed. Note the 'K1' shunting the NE coal drops which were extensive at this station. The signal box was part of the 1930s modernisation scheme which also resulted in many of the local stations on the main line being re-built. Most of them have since closed.

The man on a bike next to the down main would be in trouble nowadays! It is good to know that safety matters have an even higher profile now than ever before.

'V2' 2-6-2 No 60964 *The Durham Light Infantry*, Headingley, 11.33 am, 24.12.60, Down relief
How not to do it (1)! It is one thing not to spot a telegraph pole, but another to miss a whole clump of trees which then throw their shadows all over the train! In addition I had been watching trains at this spot since the age of 5! However, it is Christmas Eve and the sun is at its nadir.

The train has just left the short Headingley tunnel which goes under Kirkstall Lane - a name known to generations of cricket supporters. The named 'V2s' were always rare and this one makes a fine sight on the 1 in 100 gradient. Some examples were named after schools and I read recently that one headmaster declined to have his school honoured in this way. He felt that the naming ceremony would be a jamboree unbefitting his lofty ideas about education. Note the LNER coaches and the shunting neck for the goods yard; this was used by 'J21' engines for many years.

'Jubilee' 4-6-0 No 45597 *Barbados*, Wortley Junction, 12 noon, 7.8.63, 9.33 am Morecambe-Leeds; also '5MT' 4-6-0 No 45368, 11.34 am Harrogate-King's Cross
There are still four tracks along here - two for the Midland and two for the Harrogate line which curves away to the right beyond the bridge. Against the wall of millstone grit is a train of empty coal wagons, while the 'Jubilee' has a couple of six-wheel parcels vans - an arrangement not now to be found. Behind the 'Black Five' in the distance stands the switched-out Armley NE box; on the Midland, the signals which can be seen were controlled by Canal Road box which was built on a gantry straddling two tracks of the goods yard. The dreary houses surround Armley Gaol; until the early '50s there was a busy tram service going over the bridge.

'N1' 0-6-2T No 69469, Horsforth, 2.25 pm, 1.4.56, Relief Leeds Central-Knaresborough

This is a rare shot showing the success of the new BR diesel multiple units (DMUs)! When they were introduced in June 1954, places like Harrogate and Knaresborough became popular resorts for day trips from Leeds and Bradford because of the new mode of transport; a letter 'D' appeared at the top of the timetable columns to show which trains were diesels. You might be lucky enough to sit behind the driver or, if not, you had wide windows and a fast journey. Unfortunately, at busy holiday times, even nearly two years later, there weren't enough diesels to go round, especially as extras had to be run to cater for this new popularity. One result was the incongruous sight of an 'N1', just released from the Metropolis and complete with condensing gear for running on the Widened Lines to Moorgate, in the pleasant Yorkshire countryside. I don't suppose the passengers were any too happy, but perhaps they were more fortunate on the return journey. Most railway enthusiasts, of course, would see it the other way around!

Woodside box at one time controlled a siding into a quarry; in 1956 the connection was still there together with the signals, but out of use.

'3MT' 2-6-0 No 77014, Whitby West Cliff, 1.34 pm, 31.5.56

A traditional pick-up freight pauses at an NE station of fairly standard design. There are still several such stations to be found in the North East, but West Cliff and its railway have gone. The extensive point rodding indicates a large layout but it was not to last. Note the tangerine-coloured 'totems' ('hot dog'-shaped station nameplates) and the clock on the station wall.

The loco was fairly new at the time and helps to illustrate the dilemma in which BR was soon to find itself, ie with steam locos built during the '50s for services which were shortly to disappear. The result, hastened by dieselisation, meant a very short life for many of the later steam locos. This class was distinguished by the high running plate, while the tender is well designed for tender-first running, being cut back and provided with a window.

'D49' 4-4-0 No 62765 *The Goathland*, Selby, 2.46 pm, 29.9.56

This was a class well known to me from an early age and I make no other excuse than that for including it. No 62765 stands on the goods line behind Selby shed awaiting her next job - even a small town like Selby had a fair-sized shed with a coaling plant. NER slotted post signals oversee the lines behind the engine which is in 'bulled' condition including white-painted buffers. The fox above the nameplate indicates that she is a member of the 'Hunt' Class; in 1953 a member of this class had a Union Jack painted on it for the Coronation celebrations. Note the Lentz rotary cam valve gear.

Selby was popular with Leeds trainspotters as it was on the East Coast Main Line (ECML) and only 20 miles away. The road was mostly quite flat for cycling and even fairly safe in the days before roads became death-traps for cyclists and pedestrians alike. Selby station is still busy, but is sadly no longer on the main line; there is nowadays an 'old world charm' about the whole place.

'A8' 4-6-2T No 69881, Leeds City, 2.4 pm, 10.1.57

The 'A8s' were an attractive, larger NE tank used for passenger work. Note that part of the capuchon on the chimney has been lost. Early colour light signals, controlled by Leeds City East box, stand at the platform ends, and the driver observes a platelayer unadorned by a yellow safety jacket in those days. The lone carriage washer on the left is also noteworthy - I wonder how often his bucket needed replenishing. This was a low-paid laborious job but essential in the days before automation.

The line went on a long succession of bridges and embankments towards Marsh Lane. Note the rather rough wooden section of the platform. This area was swept away in the later station rebuilding.

'J50' 0-6-0T No 68988, Cardigan Road, Leeds, 8.51 am, 12.5.61

This is an unusual loco in a little-known locality. During the rebuilding of Leeds City station in 1961 it was necessary, at one stage, to sever all connection between the two halves of the railway system: City station, covering the old NE, LNW and Midland lines, and Central station, which still had an affinity to the GN and L&Y railways. As a result, a temporary re-allocation of locos took place, and you could see NER 'B16s' at Copley Hill and, as in the photo, a GN 'Submarine' breaking new ground on the NE line to Harrogate. Note the wooden hopper wagons being propelled on to the coal drops, while a lorry is being loaded underneath.

Coal merchants' staff walk down ready to look at the wagon labels and decide which wagons to unload first. They had to bear in mind the demurrage charges which would be raised if wagons were not unloaded within the free period. The labels showed the origin colliery and the grade of coal - singles, doubles, cobbles, etc. Until very recently these labels were still a legal requirement - for domestic coal at any rate.

'J6' 0-6-0 No 64203, Leeds Central, 12.59 pm, 5.8.61

I spent the whole of this lovely Summer Saturday counting passengers at Leeds Central for a census. The diminutive Station Foreman is also having a busy day, here giving orders to the driver of an old GN 'J6', locos which were still giving sterling service in the early 1960s on empty stock and pilot work. Note the trainspotters taking down details of everything that moved - nowadays they would use a small tape recorder. The bracket signals were quite distinctive at the platform ends and featured in many of Eric Treacy's photos. He was a local rail enthusiast of a high order and helped make the area well known throughout the country.

The signal box in the left background had been the cause of a small problem the previous Christmas. For the first time since it opened there would be no trains on Christmas Day, but it was found that the door could not be locked as the box had never had to be closed before. A locksmith had to be summoned to deal with it.

'3F' 0-6-0T No 47419, Wellington Street, 3.30 pm, 25.4.62
A local trip has just arrived. Note the large number of wagons in the background - yet this was just a small, insignificant corner of Wellington Street goods yard, which in turn was only one of the four large goods depots within the city of Leeds. The circular building was the engine shed for the Leeds & Thirsk Railway of 1849. In the 1960s many box vans of the type seen here were used for carrying 'sundries', which traffic formed the mainstay of the goods department at the time. Often there were only a few hundredweights of goods in a wagon, but there was a regular service between particular points which meant that the wagons moved no matter how little was in them. Large numbers of main-line freights and local trips consisted largely of this type of traffic. They had one advantage to the operator - as they were fitted with the vacuum brake they were useful in forming 'fitted heads' (the front part of otherwise non-continuously braked trains, useful for increasing automatic brake power) even if they did not make much money! Holbeck Low Level platform and the Midland main line are in the background. Note also the array of signals, including an unusual lattice-post lower quadrant on the right. Also in the background are the rather grim shapes of the gas works and Armley Gaol.

3

Leeds Hunslet East

May 1955 to March 1957

Almost before I had started my new job at Hunslet East, the 1955 ASLEF strike took place. As luck would have it there was also a rates increase at the same time, and this involved immense amounts of clerical effort as most of the increases had to be worked out manually by means of commercially produced books which had hundreds of pages of calculations - there were no pocket or even desk-type calculators in those days. I was despatched to Shipley to assist in this mammoth task. Trains were few and far between but, fortunately, they got me there and back.

Shipley was a good example of a medium-sized goods depot. Vast quantities of new dustbins were loaded in the shed for despatch to all parts of the country; they were of the galvanised type and so were very noisy. A door led straight from the shed into the office; it was on a latch and banged all day. This annoyed a fearsome dragon of a lady clerk who remonstrated with any unfortunate porter who dared to come in. It also caused an awful draught. The Goods Agent was a wild individual who charged about the place at breakneck speed. Woe betide the junior clerk who signed a letter to District Office with his own name above 'PER PRO GOODS AGENT'. This was done elsewhere but not at Shipley! The chief clerk was straight out of Dickens, sitting, as we all did, on a high stool at a sloping desk and looking sternly about him.

The rates work was boring in the extreme. This was in the days when freight was charged according to weight, distance and classification. The weights, of course, varied, but the other two could be worked out from a mileage book, and from the three classes which applied to dustbins and drums (from a total of 21 classes). I was given a piece of cardboard with three notches cut in it to correspond with the appropriate columns of the calculations book, and this sufficed to keep me occupied for nearly a fortnight. The dustbins, meanwhile, were moved by 3-ton cob (a

three-wheel mechanical horse with articulated trailer) to Leeds or Bradford, then by rigid vehicles for the longer distances. A few Stanier and Fowler Class '4' tanks provided a local passenger service of sorts.

Back at Hunslet East, after the strike, there was a wide variety of jobs:

1 Delivery office Here were written out dozens of delivery sheets each day for inwards traffic - mainly steel and storage traffic (of which more in a moment). No received sundries were dealt with at Hunslet East. A regular job was early turn Market Traffic. This involved getting up at 4.15 am for a 5.30 am start, making out delivery sheets and answering irate phone calls if the train was late. Again, as for fish, the local market trade depended on rail for such things as Guernsey tomatoes, potatoes, sprouts and year-round Covent Garden traffic. On this job you made up your time doing yet more Coal Waybills during the late morning.

2 Storage Vast quantities of traffic arrived, as at Marsh Lane, for storage. Here was dealt with Kelloggs, Horlicks, Fairy Snow washing powder (which was then new), Boots and Rakusens traffic. An unusual item was dry ice from ICI Billingham which was received in insulated containers. It was not, of course, taken up in the lift to the storage deck like the other traffic; instead it was immediately sent out for local delivery to undertakers and ice-cream firms. In some cases an onward passenger service was used which meant high-speed visits by the flamboyant types, as it seemed to us, from Leeds City Parcels in their fast vans.

3 Forwarding or Shipping Office This meant an 11.0 am start - what a luxury - and a 7 pm finish. Hunslet East dealt with large amounts of forwarded sundries as well as full wagon-loads. Perhaps the term 'sundries' should be explained. There was a choice of three types of service by freight train according to the amount of traffic. For consignments heavy or volumi-

35

nous enough to fill a wagon there was the wagon-load service, then known as Full Loads. Complete train, nowadays known as Trainload, is self-evident. The third kind was smaller items which might, perhaps, be sent by parcels train for a quicker but more expensive service. Vast quantities, though, were despatched by freight Sundries and might be anything from a small parcel to a heavy casting weighing 200 pounds. Many firms sent most of their production by Sundries.

E. J. Arnold, suppliers of those school exercise books that we all remember, sent thousands of items each week. These were liable to 'wrong loadings'. I once spent two weeks at Hunslet Lane checking on these. The Goods Agent, who was the most autocratic person I ever met, was mortified to receive criticisms of wrong loadings, for example a parcel for Leicester being sent in the Carlisle van. His answer to this was to fight fire with fire, and I was given the job of checking inwards wagons so that we could then criticise other people. I didn't find many so common sense prevailed and I was told to check the forwarded wagons. I found several types of wrong loadings but the commonest involved the E. J. Arnold traffic where numerous identical parcels with faintly-typed address labels resulted in people not bothering to check them all.

'Bad loadings' were a different problem. This was where parcels were not properly stacked and thus moved about, damaging each other. Hump shunting was ideal for this purpose!

Sundries might be crates sent to the docks for export or goods to Ireland, and all meant a lot of handling, carting (collection and delivery) and transhipment between wagons in order to provide a comprehensive, go-anywhere service. Hunslet East forwarded to all ex-LNER destinations except Scotland, while Hunslet Lane and Wellington Street covered the remainder and all inwards Sundries. Each day nearly 3,000 consignment notes were generated in total at the three depots - mainly for Sundries.

The mode of operation was that the 3-ton cobs went out from about midday to pick up from a regular, fixed round of customers; most of the deliveries had been made in the morning. Rigid 5-tonners would make the longer runs in from places like Otley and Wetherby. The vehicles then probably had items for all three depots, so went to each in turn to unload for transfer to the inevitable 10-ton box vans. On arrival at Hunslet East, the lorry weighed in and the driver then parked and brought the consignment notes to the office. Here they were given a progressive number by means of a simple spring-action stamping machine. Different coloured ink was used at each depot and the date preceded the number.

The notes were then photographed - after all, each represented revenue and all had to be accounted for in the Centralised Accounts Office at Hunslet Lane. Next a Checker located in the office scribbled the name of the allocated van into which the consignment should go. Out went the driver with his notes to 'perambulate', as it was known, round the depot dropping off parcels at various points where the staff loaded them into vans and endorsed the note with the wagon number. Some items might just go on to other road vehicles.

At hourly intervals the lad porter was sent round to fetch all the completed notes. What a job it was to get him to go out on a cold evening! In any case, being the junior he was subject to pranks by the lads outside and it was often necessary to send out a search party for him! It was essential to get the last round-up completed in good time otherwise it was a hectic rush to get finished and go home. A more senior clerk (the old Class 3) marked the consignment notes with the name of the station to which the goods should be charged, ie the nearest station, even though it might have been many miles away. Then all the notes were unceremoniously bundled into a leather satchel to go to Hunslet Lane for charging. We at the sharp end had done our job and the 9-to-5 people could sort out the paperwork tomorrow!

Wagon-load traffic was the cream of the goods department business, and at Hunslet East it consisted mainly of steel but could be almost any other commodity. Far less handling was involved (although it meant using cranes for the heavier items) and the road delivery was generally one or two lorries per wagon rather than employing many staff and road vehicles to move large numbers of small items. A mobile crane was often used, particularly if A or B type containers had to be lifted. If such a crane had to be moved from one depot to another it was a bit of a problem as they were not licenced to travel on the public roads. They were supposed to be towed by a lorry but, in practice, the crane usually followed a short distance behind the lorry - until separated at traffic lights. It then became something like a scene from a 'Carry On' film!

The office at Hunslet East was large and square with a fireplace at each corner. About 7 am on each winter's morning a porter would get a roaring fire going in one of them and then take shovels full of burning coals to the others, scattering ashes and dust everywhere. At lunchtime the older members of the staff would sit round one of the fires playing cards. The junior clerk was not allowed to join in, of course, nor to go to the pub for the traditional Christmas Eve celebrations. The Chief Clerk, of

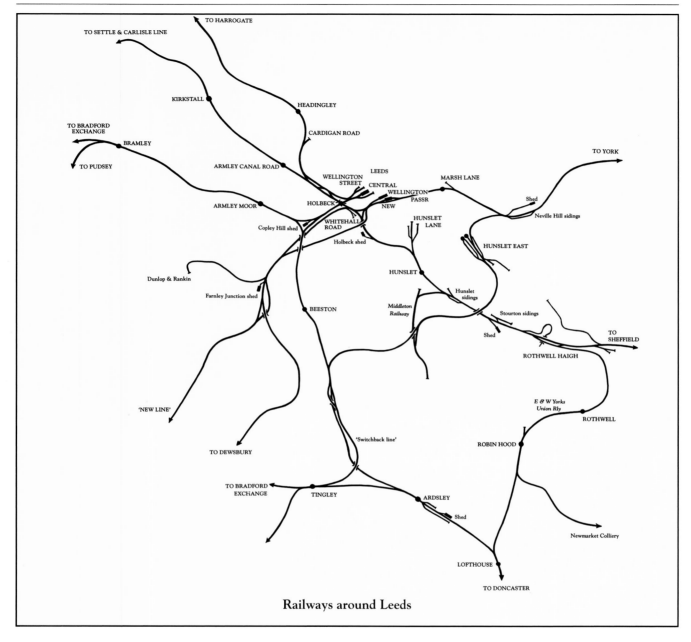

Railways around Leeds

whom I was mortally afraid, collapsed after one such occasion, scattering several of the high stools in the process. He was then escorted home to sober up. Somehow I was never afraid of him again!

One job I managed to avoid, by the skin of my teeth, was tracing. Over the years an incredible number of consignment notes, kept in pads with leather covers, was accumulated in the Muniments room at Hunslet Lane. In the event of claims for damaged or missing goods, somebody had to find the note so that the destination and wagon number details could be used. At Hunslet East the early part of Forwarding Office work involved dealing with public complaints - letters from customers, often wonderfully embossed,

had to be acknowledged and contact made with the destination by wire using the marvellous codes which enabled whole sentences to be compressed into one word. The real bore, though, in all this was the tracing.

Another job was invoicing. All full wagon loads and any consignment of a ton or more had to have an invoice. These were made out by hand, like many of the customer accounts, and sent to the destination. In some cases, especially Kelloggs, there might be only half a ton filling a 10-ton capacity van and it could be going just to Bradford, but an invoice was still necessary. This phase brought to an end my early and essential grounding in Goods Station work.

Barnsley, 3.18 pm, 23.3.58

The main point about this photo is that every single engine on the shed on this March Sunday is of Great Central origin. The yard is literally packed full. There is not an inch to spare for another engine so the surplus ones are parked further down the line. It must have been very difficult working under such conditions. Imagine the scene early next morning before first light. Practically all these engines would be steamed and moved out - smoke, steam and complicated shunting movements all over the place - but this was normal at countless sheds in steam days. It sounds fun to a rail enthusiast but was hard day-to-day work for 140 years for many men, perhaps a minority, who were not interested except as a way to make a living. The crossing gates have seen better days and hardly serve to keep people off the line or out of the shed.

'A3' 4-6-2 No 60081 *Shotover*, Leeds City, 1.3 pm, 30.12.60, 9.55 am Newcastle-Liverpool Lime Street

Leeds City as it used to be. People complain nowadays about the state of the ballast and sleepers covered with oil from the diesels, but they didn't always look very good in steam days either, as can be seen in this photo. The 'A3', one of the regulars, was about to be replaced by two rebuilt 'Patriots' (Nos 45528 and 45535) for the journey on to Liverpool, and stands at the west end of the train, indicating an inward journey via Wetherby. Had the train arrived via Headingley, the loco would have been at the other end of the train. Now there is no choice but to travel via York. Other regular 'A3s' on this work were *Gainsborough*, *Columbo* and *Harvester*. At one time *Tranquil* could be seen. I always thought this was a marvellous name for such a lovely loco. I suppose it was the contrast between the name and the effort required in moving 12 coaches up the 1 in 100 through Headingley! The Mark I stock carries a mixture of liveries.

'4MT' 2-6-4T No 42139, Leeds City, 1.36 pm, 1.2.61, 7.40 am Bristol-Bradford Forster Square

The end of platforms 5 and 6 was a popular venue for spotters - you could see everything in the 'Wellington' station, ie the Midland part, as well as the west end of the 'New' station, covering NE and LNW services.

These attractive locos were a Fairburn development of the Stanier Class '4' tank, and worked heavy trains on to Bradford after a 'Jubilee' or 'Scot' had brought them in from the South (No 45612 in this case), but it was a pretty flat bit of line. Sometimes the trains were double headed and I well remember the ancient driver of an equally ancient L&Y 2-4-2 tank yanking open the long regulator and hoping for the best and that the other engine was in better fettle!

Note the GPO vehicle; these worked for many years directly from the platform to the sorting office in nearby Infirmary Street. An early DMU is at the platform in the distance and the signals still look 'Midland' even though converted to upper quadrant. Notable also is the extensive area for coaching stock on the right, including provision for cleaning as indicated by the raised footboards. This part of the station is still busy though now devoted entirely to parcels traffic.

'4F' 0-6-0 No 43931, Kirkstall, 2.16 pm, 25.4.62, Up Class F
The '4F' is hauling a train of empty coke hoppers which have high sides, the point being that coke is light in weight so you can build up the sides of existing wagons or build new in that form to carry large volumes but without too heavy a weight. Iron ore wagons have completely the opposite problem and there is a danger of overloading; in some cases wagons have been built with low sides for this reason. The tracks in the left foreground are the slow lines descending from a bridge where they crossed the fast lines, enabling stopping passenger trains to be kept clear at the approaches to Leeds.

Just behind the loco a little saddle tank is shunting in Kirkstall Power Station. It was very common for many years to see such locos. Today power stations do not need locos of any sort as the train engines of 'merry-go-round' (MGR) coal trains do the work.

'J94' 0-6-0ST No 68011, Beeston Junction, 4.28 pm, 18.2.61, 3.35 pm Class K Hunslet East-Ardsley
It is late on a winter Saturday afternoon and the light has nearly gone. I was returning from a photo session at Horbury when I heard this train in the distance; I had to wait several minutes even after it came into sight as it was moving at a snail's pace, frequently slipping to a stand. The small loco and the train crew were overwhelmed by the heavy load but battled gamely on towards Ardsley; the fireman, nonetheless, looks relaxed. Perhaps he had given up the unequal struggle. I suppose they had little choice as, no doubt, their turn of duty would be finished when they arrived at Ardsley and, if they threw in the towel and requested assistance, it would mean even more delay. The train consists mainly of vanfits of sundries after a normal Saturday working day. Whether it reached Ardsley without being rescued I do not know, but they certainly did their best.

These 'J94' tanks replaced the ex-GN 'J52s' and, to some extent, the 'J50' 'Submarines'.

'J39' 0-6-0 No 64760, Stourton, 7.32 pm, 27.5.60, 7.30 pm Class H Hunslet East-Ardsley
One of those lucky shots! The '4F' on the Midland main line below is just right. On the top line, now disappeared, the 'J39', blowing off steam and displaying Class H lamps, labours away from Hunslet East with GN traffic for the south. Most of this long line of vans will contain small amounts of sundries traffic. In the background is Skelton Grange Power Station which had its own fleet of steam shunting engines to deal with huge amounts of coal off the Midland line. Then, as now, barges also brought in a lot of coal. The NE line to Neville Hill from Hunslet East is off the picture to the left. Nearby is Waddingtons, home of the 'Monopoly' board game.

Copley Hill Shed, 1.43 pm, 12.5.61
Shed views are always interesting if there is plenty of activity, but this smoky scene shows what a problem they caused in the local area. A 'B16' represents an unusual visitor, due to the rebuilding of Leeds City station causing locos to be away from their usual haunts. Standard tank No 80117 was probably there for the same reason. The Stanier tank on the extreme right was one of a small number at Copley Hill; I noted them on parcels trains, replacing ex-GN 'J6s'. There are plenty of brake vans and coal trucks standing about; the coaling plant is at the far end of the shed. The carriage sheds dominate the left-hand side of the picture. Note the concrete signal post in the foregrond and the old grounded coach bodies on the left behind the locos. The main line to King's Cross is marked by the bracketed signal. The whole of this site is now occupied by a factory.

'T1' 4-8-0T No 69921, Gascoigne Wood, 2.28 pm, 3.4.59
This was the hump engine at Gascoigne Wood and it always seemed odd to have such a yard out in the country. Nowadays it is the location of one of Britain's busiest collieries, part of the Selby coalfield which extends a long way underground; this is where the coal is loaded into numerous MGR trains each day.
 The 4-8-0T wheel arrangement was very unusual, especially for a tank engine - you would normally expect another pair of wheels under the bunker. The 'T1' had extensive tanks and coal bunker which would enable the loco to keep going for a long shift before returning to Selby shed. Note the shunting pole on the rear buffer and the shunter who didn't need to wear a yellow high-visibility vest in those days - the baggy black uniform and the cap are typical of the period.

'1F' 0-6-0T No 41779 and 'J50' 0-6-0T No 68974, Doncaster Shed, 1.37 pm, 2.12.56
This was a normal, large-shed scene of the 1950s, apart from the obvious visitor from another railway. There are long lines of loco coal wagons, many wooden, waiting to go to the coaling plant. Other wagons, for loco ash, stand in a sub-level pit and are ready for loading. Surely this was one of the filthier jobs and explains, to some extent, the need to move away from steam.
 The contrasting locos were built in 1878 and 1926 respectively. The Midland '1F' tank was the only one with this type of dome that I managed to catch on film. It has no vacuum pipe but boasts adequate steps for the shunters to ride on. The 'J50' 'Submarine' was a very common type at Doncaster. It is hard to imagine a greater contrast in styles for locos designed for the same job, although perhaps foreign railways managed it.

'A3' 4-6-2 No 60069 *Sceptre*, 9.20 am relief Glasgow St Enoch-St Pancras, and '4MT' 2-6-0 No 43117, 1.58 pm (Suns) Bradford Forster Square-Birmingham, Kirkstall, 2.17 pm, 31.3.61

On a four-track line you always hoped for a race, whether you were on a train and could enjoy the excitement for several miles, or whether you were at the lineside and might just be in the right spot to take a photo. I suppose if you spent as many hours as I did around Kirkstall, you were bound to be lucky eventually. In this case I was even more fortunate as it was a Sunday. The 'A3s' were improbable locos to replace the 'Scots', but welcome nevertheless. Although the Ivatt 2-6-0s were not a particularly attractive loco, in my view, they did do a lot of work in this area.

Over the wall on the left is the Leeds-Liverpool canal, one of the few still carrying goods after the war. It enabled me to walk along the towpath to reach otherwise remote spots on the main line.

'Britannia' 4-6-2 No 70037 *Hereward the Wake*, Beeston Junction, 4.19 pm, 15.6.63, 4.10 pm Leeds Central-Cleethorpes

We are 182 miles from King's Cross, and the switchback line to Tingley with its flying junction has now gone. There were trains at one time which made a roundabout journey from Leeds Central via Tingley and Batley to Wakefield. On the main line the Cleethorpes was a time-honoured train, although the ex-GCR 'Directors', used in former days, seemed more appropriate than a 'Britannia'. However, *Hereward the Wake* does have express lamps up which makes it look a little better.

This location was one of my favourites in steam days. The bridge formed a good backdrop and trains were usually working hard up the gradient. 'A4s' were in use on the London trains along here until the 1960s.

'4MT' 2-6-4T No 42138, Shipley, 9.31 am, 10.6.55, Leeds City-Bradford Forster Square local (special service)
Not many trains ran during the 1955 Rail Strike but this was one of them. It was, otherwise, a typical local stopping train of the period with non-corridor compartment stock and a commendably clean loco. On the left is Shipley Goods depot with the ubiquitous B-type containers on two types of wagon - one is a flat, but the other shows the not uncommon practice of using a high goods which should have been kept for its proper purpose. It was, however, difficult to control such things in the days before computers. Sometimes it was just a case of taking the easy option, ie grabbing whatever was to hand. Behind is what appears to be a mobile crane. The office was at the far end of the sheds.

This is still a busy passenger line with trains from Bradford to Ilkley and Skipton. The passenger station, which the train has just left, has the distinction that it had platforms in use on two sides of the triangle in 1955, but now on all three.

'D49' 4-4-0 No 62753 *The Belvoir*, Armley, 6.6 pm, 15.6.55, 5.30 pm Harrogate-Leeds City
This was one result of the 1955 strike which had just ended - every inch of siding had to be used to stable goods and passenger stock. Note the various sorts of fitted vans, the mainstay for sundries traffic over many years. A more normal use for these sidings was for storing coaching stock for excursions; on Summer Saturdays many trains were worked to Leeds Central for holiday specials. The 'Hunt' is working a typical Harrogate local and is just nearing the point where it will run alongside the Midland main line before joining it on the approach to the next stop, Holbeck Low Level. This was an important changing point although virtually unknown to the local population, lost as it was amongst grim industrial backstreets.

'4F' 0-6-0 No 43987, Holbeck Low Level, 3.0 pm, 28.6.58, 2.55 pm Leeds City-Bradford Forster Square
Holbeck station has only a week to go before closure, a sad day indeed for the many trainspotters who frequented its platforms and ran up and down the stairs to catch everything on both levels. The '4F' makes quite a fine sight on a local service that has long ago disappeared, but there are now through trains from King's Cross to Bradford using the Midland route from Leeds and passing this spot. On the left is the spur to the high level and Leeds Central with a 'Hunt' going up to work the Harrogate portion of a London train. The line to the right of the signal gantry was known as the 'Independent', indicating its pre-nationalisation status as a line in no-man's-land between two railway companies where trains were handed over. When I worked in the Trains Office, two years later, there were still problems when parcels vans were exchanged here; the firemen refused to unhook their locos, considering that a shunter should have been provided to do this dirty job.

'D49' 4-4-0 No 62717 *Banffshire*, Hull Paragon, 7.47 am, 23.2.57, 7.50 am to York
Banffshire is apparently a long way from home although sporting a local shedplate. To obtain this early morning shot meant getting up at 4.15 am in Leeds but, as that was my normal time during the week for the early turn market job, it was not a problem - why not just get up at the same time on Saturday? The pleasant cross-country run to York via Market Weighton is today but a memory, as is 'G5' No 67282 at the other platform. Paragon station was very busy with locals to Hornsea and Withernsea as well as the York trains. Nowadays there is still quite a good service, especially to Doncaster, Leeds and Bridlington.

'B1' 4-6-0 No 61144, New Holland Pier, 9.16 am, 23.2.57, 9.47 am to Cleethorpes
It is a cold morning, with snow to come later, and the steam heating leaks in a couple of places, but the fine clean loco has only a short journey to make. The paddle-steamer from Hull has arrived at the end of the ramp to the right but there are still many minutes to wait before the 'B1' departs, perhaps to allow for delays on the river. Now the Humber Bridge obviates this connection but there is a good local service of DMUs in the Grimsby area. Note the run-round facilities for both platforms and the two wagons at the river end.

Generally, this photo illustrates BR's commitment at that time to provide a service linking the important towns and cities on each side of the Humber despite lack of the proper equipment for the job. A 'B1' was hardly ideal, being capable of greater things and needing to run round at each end of the journey.

'Jubilee' 4-6-0 No 45618 *New Hebrides*, Engine Shed Junction, Leeds, 4.26 pm, 10.8.63, 7.15 am Paignton-Bradford Forster Square relief
It is fairly late on a Saturday afternoon but passengers in a rake of LMS stock have only just got back to the West Riding after a holiday in Devon. The rather exotically named loco no doubt took over from a GWR 'Hall' at Bristol several hours ago but appears to have a fair amount of coal left and has, undoubtedly, changed crews a number of times on the way. The 'Black Five' in the background is on the LNW line from Manchester. It is only in recent years that this line has been taken out of use and such trains now travel via Whitehall Junction. Under the bridge is considerable smoke at Holbeck engine shed, known to locals as 'Ninevah' after the name of the road passing the shed. Both the shed and the junction, on the Midland main line, are still in use today. It could also be said that, despite the overwhelming use of the car, such holiday trains thankfully still run. And a good thing too!

'Black Five' 4-6-0 No 44830, Ardsley, 12.21 pm, 18.3.61, 9.35 am Leicester Central-Leeds Central excursion

This was a football excursion when, unusually, Elland Road was used as a neutral ground for a Cup Tie. As can be seen, there were extensive sidings on both sides of the main Doncaster-Leeds line at Ardsley. There was a large engine shed in the distance, home at one time to ex-GC 4-6-0 *Immingham*. Note the gas lamps, and the passengers who, perhaps, had walked across from the outskirts of Leeds, only a short distance across the fields. Hunslet East was served by trips from Ardsley, usually hauled by ancient 'J50' 'Submarine' tanks.

Behind me the GN line to Bradford Exchange via Morley Top turned off. For many years this was the preferred route for the Bradford portions of London trains, attached or detached at Wakefield Westgate. Some wandered along the Dewsbury branch to provide the wool towns with a service to 'the Smoke'. Later the line round the back of Copley Hill shed was used, but this has now been cut, much to the chagrin of Bradfordians who must now perforce travel via their rival city, Leeds. Now the M62 motorway cuts across here and Ardsley station and yards are no more.

4

Other people's railways
April 1957 to April 1959

There was a gap in my BR service for two years due to National Service, but it gave me an opportunity to have a look at railways in other parts of the country and see how they did things. Bearing in mind the pre-nationalisation, if not actually pre-Grouping, atmosphere which then prevailed, it was not surprising that I found much of interest in my travels. These were entirely in Britain as I was keen not to go abroad. At any other time I would have been very happy to see foreign railways but, due to the 1955 Modernisation programme, it was obvious that the days of steam on

BR were numbered so there was no time to lose.

This chapter, then, is a broad brush stroke view of railways in places where I didn't work but found many unusual and photogenic items. I have cheated a little as regards dates. Not all the photos fall within the period under review but I have tried to select photos to illustrate particular features. Certainly there was plenty of steam interest in the late 1950s but the dieselisation process was gathering pace. On the freight side, the major changes were still to come, particularly the main oil train contracts, MGR and Freightliner workings.

Ulster Railways 0-6-0 No 13, York Road, Belfast, 12.54 pm, 10.6.61
When is a '4F' not a '4F'? On this occasion it is the Ulster version running on 5 ft 3 in gauge. Note the quaint outside-frame tender with the metal number plate on the back and a wooden board to help retain the coal. The cab has a single-line tablet catcher and the shunter has adequate metal steps to stand on whilst the pilot is moving around the yard. There is a gateway into the yard, which appears to belong to the Engineers Department.

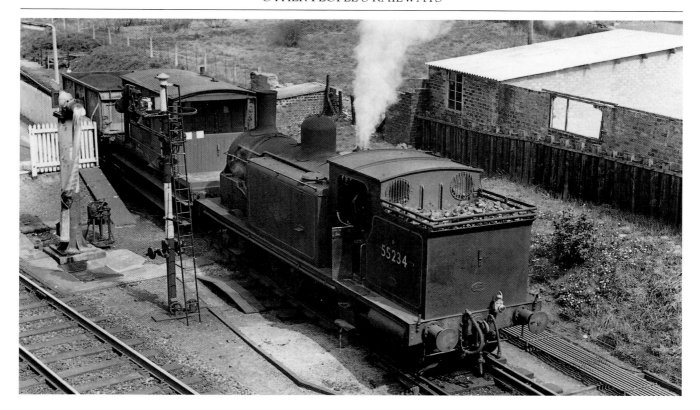

Caledonian '294' Class 0-6-0 No 57661, Dumfries, 9.46 am, 4.5.62, Up Class J

From Ireland to Scotland. On at earlier visit, in 1956, our first sight of things Scottish had been at Dumfries. Our train ground to a halt near the loco shed in torrential rain, but a few yards away stood 57600 of another 'Caley' goods engine class. It was a wonderful sight even though the conditions were bad, and was a reminder that the Celtic regions had a very special character in those days. Soon after arriving at the station, we were treated to the sight of the Station Inspector running the full length of the platform, still in heavy rain, in an attempt to prevent the driver of a 'Black Five', on a freight train, from stopping for water at the end of the platform. No doubt this was due to other trains, like ours, being held up outside Dumfries. Unfortunately the driver won and the bag was in the tender before the irate Inspector got there!

This 1962 photograph was a lucky find near the point where the Stranraer and Glasgow lines diverged to the west of Dumfries. The train consists of a wide variety of commodities for a country area - chemicals, cement and the usual coal empties and vans. The fine-looking loco is in clean condition with a nice chimney, unlike some 'Caley' engines which were rather disfigured by stove-pipes; practical, no doubt, but not aesthetically pleasing.

The train crew are enjoying the fine spring weather. Now, of course, the Stranraer line is no more, but oil traffic is still dealt with at Maxwelltown.

Caledonian '2F' 0-6-0 No 57396, Stirling South, 5.43 pm, 31.7.56

I have included this photograph, dating from the earlier 1956 visit, mainly because it is a pleasant scene, summing up a more leisurely way of life in the days of steam when pre-Grouping locos of fine appearance were still to be found. I particularly liked the design of the tenders on these locos, although I don't suppose things were quite so nice when working tender first in cold or wet weather - notice, however, the furled waterproof sheet on the cab. The coal is pulled well forward and the tender has a screw coupling.

The shed was Stirling's Caledonian depot; there was also a North British shed. This sort of duplication disappeared long ago.

Caledonian '2P' 0-4-4T No 55234, Lockerbie, 12.30 pm, 4.5.62

It was always a pleasure to look over a bridge parapet at a station and see a steam engine below; this one announced its presence from afar as it was blowing off steam. I suppose the lack of steam and semaphore signals makes it less obvious, nowadays, that trains are about, but the growl of a hard-working diesel can sometimes make up for it. The loco has a typical 'Caley' stove-pipe chimney and the driver's door is open. The filler cap for the water can be seen on the side tank. Note the rather odd signal post with an off-set, shortened arm for the main line (no doubt to compensate for awkward sighting) and a small arm for shunting purposes. The water crane has its 'bag' - the floppy hose that goes into the tender - neatly stowed and there is a fire crate next to it to stop the water from freezing in winter. The end of the platform has a neat fence. This was just a chance shot, but with quite a lot of interesting items only revealed by later examination.

'Crab' 2-6-0 No 42919, Newton Stewart, 2.28 pm, 24.6.63, Up freight
A photo full of railway atmosphere. The 'Crab' has been recessed so that my train, the 1.40 pm Stranraer Harbour-Dumfries and hauled by 'Black Five' No 44957, can pass. Note the small hole in the tender with water leaking. I had this photo published in *Rail News* recently and asked readers to write in with news of the present whereabouts of the driver and fireman. I received several replies even nearly 30 years after the photo was taken and long after the line, station and trains had disappeared. The signal on the left has a smoke deflector underneath; the other has, as well as a slender lattice post, a fine finial on top. The lamp post is of fine design.

'3MT' 2-6-2T No 40011, Banff, 5.17 pm, 23.6.59, 5.25 pm to Tillynaught Junction
Scotland had more than its share of attractive branch lines but not many had a terminus with an all-over roof. This always made a station appear special but could be a problem for the photographer unless he had a flash unit - not common in the 1950s. Note the oil lamp cases and wooden station nameboard on the platform screen. Just across the river was another branch terminus, at Macduff. That line made its way to Aberdeen by a much more direct route than the one from Banff, which set off in a westerly direction towards Keith.

North British 'J36' 0-6-0 No 65346, Alford, Aberdeenshire, 1.8 pm, 24.6.59
The unusual feature about this photo, taken at the terminus of a little-known branch, is the van with its door standing open. I have occasionally heard the term 'road van' used but this is the only case where I managed to capture one. Sundries could be loaded into the van along the 'road', ie at intermediate stations. It also illustrates the use of the term 'road' in relation to a railway line, still often used by railwaymen; 'waiting for the road' means awaiting clearance of a signal, for example. When I was a clerk in a goods office, people could bring in a parcel to send by goods train, as they still can for a passenger service; they could also pay cash if they didn't have an account. The loco is recently ex-works and is standing at the old passenger station; the goods shed is in the background.

I had to beat a hasty retreat shortly after taking this photo when I saw the train crew rapidly approaching from the signal box, where they had doubtless been for a cup of tea. They obviously thought I was trespassing. I didn't wait to find out!

GNSR 'Z5' 0-4-2T No 68192, Aberdeen Docks, 10.10 am, 27.3.57
This interesting picture shows how fish used to be dealt with at Aberdeen. I was very lucky to find this loco in the dock area but didn't have time to wait around to see if the same personal service was provided elsewhere in the docks - the loco has brought a van to the fish merchant's very door so that it can be loaded. There were, of course, very few locos of this wheel arrangement, and you had to go looking for them. A bit of luck helped as well! The dome is quite remarkable - it would not have disgraced an engine of twice the size.

North British 'J88' 0-6-0T Nos 68324 and 68354, Polmont, 1.52 pm, 31.7.56
It really is incredible to think that such delightful locos were still around in the 1950s! The most notable accoutrements are, of course, the tall chimneys and block buffers. There cannot have been many locos with such primitive buffing gear - no frills for common shunting engines in those parts. Note the differing bunkers - the one on the right, when filled with coal, results in the rear windows being blocked. In common with many Scottish locos, these have large numerals; it was always exciting to see 'Black Fives' in the West Riding sporting large numbers, as this was indicative of their being visitors from over the Border. The bare wooden shed was unusual and rather forbidding in appearance - it is hardly the material you would expect to be used for a loco shed.

Caledonian '2P' 0-4-4T Nos 55199 and 55198, Inverness, 3.41 pm, 2.5.61
This equally delightful pair were standing near Inverness station. The engines' numbers are consecutive but they have different BR totems on the side tanks; the 'Caley' brake pumps are evident next to the cab of 55199. Many railways employed 0-4-4 tanks and it is difficult to think of one that was unattractive. They were a joy to behold on a country branch, and these Scottish examples could be seen on local freight trips as well as on branch-line and station pilot duties. Note the number of lamps on the locos - five can be seen, and there were probably more round the back. The lorry behind No 55199 seems to be rather close to the line. . .

North British 'J35' 0-6-0 No 64515, Haddington, 4.9 pm, 25.6.59

This branch was not very far off the beaten track, being only 17 miles from Edinburgh and located on the A1 road. The size of the train tells its own story, although there are several wagons in the yard. Note that the side lamps on the brake van have not yet been transferred to the other end ready for the return journey. These showed a white light forward and red to the rear, giving a total of three red rearwards including the tail lamp. The driver kept an eye on the white lights whilst en route, in accordance with the Rules, to ensure that the train was complete. The signalman looked for the red lamps, and 'Train out of Section' could not be belled until he had seen such a lamp on each train. This could, however, be a problem where a train went into a siding before reaching the box. Now, in the days of fully-fitted trains and power boxes, many signalmen do not even see the trains at all.

The practice of retaining the station platform after closure (1949 in this case) seemed to be fairly common in Scotland.

Caledonian '812' Class 0-6-0 No 57594, Muir of Ord, 12.46 pm, 19.6.59

The hot summer of 1959 was a boon for photographers but, unfortunately, my camera was causing problems. Luckily it did not spoil this peaceful scene in the far North of Scotland, where the railway really did provide a lifeline in these parts and not just in bad weather. This train has a wide variety of traffics and there is more freight on the left-hand side of the platform. Note the typical Highland Railway footbridge and the driver looking down the train for the 'right away'. The line north of Inverness had its own special character in steam days - 'Caley' 4-4-0s were always worth seeing and even the ubiquitous 'Black Fives' somehow seemed different.

Caledonian '294' Class 0-6-0 No 57679, Stirling, 4.10 pm, 4.5.61, Down Class J

This is an area well known for seed potatoes, and large quantities were conveyed by rail. A noteworthy feature is that the first two vans are sheeted, indicating leaking roofs. The sheets each had their own numbers for control purposes - it was even more difficult to control sheets and ropes than wagons, but just as important if you couldn't move the traffic until you had them. Chocks for securing cars on wagons were also a problem. Those sorts of items tended to be thrown on the ground and forgotten.

The driver's door is open at the side of his cab. On the right a 'Black Five' is about to depart with a short train. The fine metal railings on the left-hand platform guard a subway ramp.

'Princess Coronation' 4-6-2 No 46252 *City of Leicester*, Stirling, 5.46 pm, 4.5.61, Up fish
In any of their guises, whether 'Duchesses' or 'Cities', Stanier's 'Pacifics' could look just as magnificent on freight as on passenger. Obviously they were not often used on freight, but the Aberdeen fish was one such job. Note the length of the train, seen just a few years before this traffic disappeared from rail. The signal on the right is rather unusual as the arm is well down the post, which is of lattice construction, a pleasant style adopted by the Caledonian Railway. The 'Caley' shed was still in use at this time.

'Royal Scot' 4-6-0 No 46166 *London Rifle Brigade***, Forteviot, 12.4 pm, 16.4.64, 12.35 pm Perth-Carlisle parcels**
I have included this photo mainly because of the smoke effect, but 'Scots' were quite a favourite class and I remember the first ones to be rebuilt during the war and working from Holbeck. The first van of the train is of LNER origin, but many of the others would not be amiss at the same place today. The only other item of interest is the author's mode of transport on the right. Not quite up to the standard of Ivo Peters's famous Bentley!

'3F' 0-6-0T No 47269, Durran Hill, 2.55 pm, 4.5.62, Up Class K

Moving south into England, we arrive at Durran Hill Junction, Carlisle. This sort of photo has been seen elsewhere but I include it to show the considerable amount of points, signals, etc, involved in serving marshalling yards which were later replaced by the large new yards of the '60s. Now the 'new' yards themselves have almost gone. The Midland 'Jinty' is passing a box built by the same company. Next to the engine is an empty cattle truck and on the front of the loco is a circular target number denoting the identity of the local working. There is a lot of activity in the background. Happily, although the yards have now disappeared, the Settle & Carlisle line in the foreground is still with us.

'Black Five' 4-6-0 No 45259, Dent, 12.25 pm, 13.4.64

One of those lucky shots. It was raining and cold - not unusual on the Settle & Carlisle line - and I was about to give up when this cavalcade appeared. No doubt they were going to Scotland for scrapping, but unfortunately I did not catch the numbers of the other locos. Maybe I can use the weather as an excuse, but I very rarely missed recording such details. It was part of the skill of photographing fast-moving trains and one I find more difficult with advancing years.

This location has become very popular in recent years but, in 1964, the S&C was still struggling on towards an uncertain future. There was, of course, the compensating factor of quite a lot of day-to-day steam about instead of the odd special or DMU of today. Note the snow fencing on the hillside above the station.

'4F' 0-6-0 No 44197, Long Preston, 10.30 am, 13.4.64, Down Class 9

I have never been able to solve the mystery of this incident, photographed at Long Preston, just south of Settle Junction. The '4F' was propelling its train, at considerable speed, along the down main and soon disappeared into the distance towards Giggleswick. The question is - was it a normal, authorised, daily occurrence, or perhaps a move allowed under ballast train conditions? Certainly it was, and is, unusual to see such a long-distance propelling movement.

The veranda of the Midland box sports such domestic implements as a brush and shovel. The glass case on the platform was for an oil lamp and between it and the box there is a sleeper-built coal bunker. If this was for the use of the signalman, it seems to be rather a long way from the box and perhaps explains the need for the brush! The siding on the left appears to be little used, while the platelayer standing on the up main seems unconcerned by the whole business. Finally, the tender cab is a noteworthy and necessary item in this part of the world although, when running tender first, the driver cannot have had a good view.

L&YR '27' Class 0-6-0 No 52429, Lostock Hall Shed, 6.5 pm, 15.5.60
Moving south again to Lostock Hall, Preston, it is a Sunday afternoon but this ancient L&Y 0-6-0 is in steam. Perhaps it has been working a weekend Engineers train or is being prepared for one. I was reading the Wakefield Control Log one day in 1961 and came across an item regarding an L&Y 0-6-0 which disgraced itself by running out of water at Thornhill. It was no fun for the fireman, who had to throw out the fire, but it was probably his fault in the first place. At a distance of 30 years, however, the incident appears rather endearing and the sort of thing that might happen to Thomas the Tank Engine.

There is quite a contrast between the 0-6-0 and the more modern, if less attractive, 'WDs' on each side. These large locos were the workhorses of the area in the 1950s and early 1960s, and I remember them particularly on heavy coal trains, almost entirely consisting of 16-ton mineral wagons, from Yorkshire to Lancashire. By the end of steam, in 1968, the '8Fs' had become better known in this part of the world.

'J6' 0-6-0 Nos 64247, 64220 and 64244, Boston, 2.9 pm, 8.9.56
On the other side of the country, here is a quiet scene on a late summer Saturday; the locos have been damped down for the weekend after Saturday morning work, which was usual at the time. The leading loco has also been cleaned up, perhaps for passenger work. My journey to Boston was along the now closed line from Lincoln and, although flat, it was a lovely run, particularly behind a 'J6'. The line followed the River Witham for several miles, with East Midlands anglers spaced out along the bank for a large competition. Seen from afar, the beautiful golden tower of 'Boston Stump' was unmistakable. Other locos on shed were Nos 68557 and 69284.

'O4' 2-8-0 No 63582, Bidston, 12.9 pm, 3.11.56
The GC presence on Merseyside was always a source of interest to me, particularly that on the Wirral side of the river, and this robust Robinson workhorse does not really seem at home here. One of the main points of the photo, however, is the fascinating method for dealing with the loco coal, seen in the background. It seems to be a classic case of labour-intensive work, involving two men stooping to shovel coal out of the 21-ton wagons and into narrow-gauge trucks of unusual design before a further move to the coaling plant.

'Jubilee' 4-6-0 No 45571 *South Africa*, **Wigan North Western, 1.9 pm, 18.6.55, 8.30 am Euston-Blackpool Central**
There's a large expanse of tracks and pointwork, but the photo serves to illustrate a traditional local gas works siding on the far side. Many of the wagons are wooden. I didn't know the area so I am unaware of the method of serving the siding. Probably it was a train-load from a nearby colliery, of which there were several in those days. It is impossible to tell the type of unloading, but it could have been side tippling; in some parts of the country end doors were popular, denoted by a diagonal white stripe on the side of the wagon. Other methods were the use of a grab or merely shovelling.

Wigan was a popular venue for impoverished young Yorkshire spotters as it was the nearest point on the West Coast Main Line. The lines next to the gasworks are those of the L&Y coming in from Manchester in the distance to Wallgate station away to the left.

'Compound' 4-4-0 No 41121, Crewe, 5.45 pm, 13.8.52
This is one of my earliest photos, taken with an old pre-war folding Kodak camera. This was a typical family camera and had two speeds, 1/25 and 1/50 - not very good for taking moving trains, which was what I wanted to do at the time. This was the case with many young aspiring photographers. Perhaps we would have been better advised to start with stationary shots of trains in interesting station locations instead of trying to be Eric Treacys straight away. This photo could at one time have entered into the discussion of how long after nationalisation the old insignia remained - however, there have been many cases to beat this one. The lamp on the smokebox says that it is a local passenger train, but I recorded it as Empty Coaching Stock as it stood at the signal for a long time and there were no passengers on board.

'Jubilee' 4-6-0 No 45571 *South Africa*, **Betley Road, 4.36 pm, 26.6.60, 12.45pm (Suns) Euston-Blackpool**
South Africa again, on a sweltering June Sunday when the era of pre-electrification was drawing to a close. Numerous Engineers trains were around and bridges were being raised to accommodate the wires. Here the station has been removed but Betley Road lives to this day in numerous logs as a timing point south of Crewe. The signal box is at the other side of the bridge.

I failed to get a photo of a newly-painted 'Wessie' 0-8-0 on a ballast train earlier as it was standing at an inaccessible spot nearby. I could see it from the road but several fields and barbed wire fences intervened. It was a fine loco on a lovely morning but, unfortunately, the old saying 'discretion is the better part of valour' seemed a good idea at the time. Now I count it amongst a dozen or so occasions where a bit of perseverance or haste would have left fewer regrets.

'Crab' 2-6-0 No 42888, Silverdale, 5.44 pm, 25.6.60, Empty stock of 5.10 pm (SO) Stoke-Silverdale
This was a virtually unknown spot, at least for anyone who lived outside the locality. There were very few passenger trains left running between Stoke and Silverdale and this one arrived tender first; there were full run-round, signalling and level crossing facilities at this small station but, of course, no turntable. A set of stock is stabled in the yard and all is peace and tranquility; as could be expected when there was such a sparse service and plenty of Potteries buses about, there were few passengers for such a train service. The colliery, however, still exists and is now served from the WCML via the Madeley Chord.

'4F' 0-6-0 No 43855, Berkeley Road, 6.15 pm, 28.6.60, 5.15 pm Bristol-Birmingham
On seeing this photo, a friend commented that only the Midland would have a siding trailing straight off a major main line to a cattle dock a short distance away, as on the left of this photo! Certainly this spot is a long way from the better-known Midland stamping grounds, but the atmosphere is evident in abundance. The line still went into the warehouse and there were lamp-cases for paraffin lights on the platform. Several people have alighted from the train and luggage is being dealt with, making it a typical English country station scene of the steam era. The '4F' had a long journey, calling at nearly all stations to Birmingham.

Out of sight to the right is the GW line to Lydney; a GW push-and-pull train awaited connections before the journey over the Severn bridge, which was later demolished after being severely damaged by a barge. Today there are just the two tracks of the NE/SW main line together with the station pub, but freight trains still run to Berkeley on the branch.

L&YR '27' Class 0-6-0 No 52119, Holywell Junction, 4.29 pm, 2.6.61
The North Wales main line of the LNWR 30 years ago was a very busy railway, not least from a freight point of view. The four tracks were hard pressed, at times, coping with the traffic. During holiday periods there was a constant procession of 'Black Five'-hauled passenger trains. This L&Y 0-6-0 seems rather out of place here but they performed great feats in many parts of the North. No 52119 is stretched to its limits in moving a very heavy load. Its sparse cab must have made life hard for the crew in bad weather.

'9F' 2-10-0 No 92024, Luton Midland Rd, 11.40 am, 9.4.58

We approach London via the Midland Main Line at Luton. These 'Franco-Crosti'-boilered locos were fascinating, although some would say not very attractive. This was the only photo I managed to get from the chimney side. One of the many 'fish that got away' was at Mirfield, when a 'Crosti', rebuilt to normal working, passed but I was not in a position to take a photo of it.

There was considerable freight through Luton and, of course, the 'Garratts' were regulars for many years. Note the two sheeted hoppers next to the loco, which presumably contained lime. The wooden 'high goods' wagons in the goods yard were standard open wagons for many years. The sides were not particularly high but the name pointed out the difference between them and low or medium wagons. The platform line on the left is buffer-stopped for trains starting or terminating at Luton.

'N2' 0-6-2T No 69594, Wood Green, 2.54 pm, 25.5.57

I always found it intriguing to see an obvious passenger loco working a freight train. The 'N2s' were the mainstay of the King's Cross suburban services for many years and it still seems strange to visit the Cross and find them gone. Wood Green has changed a lot in recent times, quite apart from the wires going up; note the substantial buildings and footbridge. There is still some freight on this line, mainly stone and cement, but none of the mixed goods trains which you could see everywhere in the '50s.

'J52' 0-6-0ST No 68875, Canonbury, 2.16 pm, 14.8.56

This was an afternoon of pure joy. Whilst visiting Hackney Downs station I noticed another line crossing underneath with a constant procession of short freight trains - it was, of course, the North London. Canonbury proved to be a good spot for photography on this line. The electrics from Broad Street to Richmond used the platforms to the left, but those to the right were utterly abandoned. The goods trips were, of course, still aligned to their pre-1923 origins. Those from the GN produced 'J50s' and 'J52s', the Midland mainly 'Jinties' and 'Crabs'. The GN passenger services from Broad Street, purely rush hour, then appeared. These had the inevitable 'N2s', which brought in their empty stock before returning laden with commuters for the Northern Heights. The splitting distant signals above the loco indicate the turn off to Finsbury Park whence this train has come. I sometimes refer to this location as the Hanging Gardens of Canonbury!

GER 'J15' 0-6-0 No 65455, Epping, 1.17 pm, 27.4.57
This photo is mainly intended to demonstrate that Epping was, from a railway point of view, not just a place at the end of the Central line. It is well known that a GE tank worked the Epping to Ongar push-and-pull; this has been well documented and was, of course, the reason for my visit. The 'J15' was a bonus, standing outside the small loco shed which appeared to be fairly new although very smoke blackened where the locos entered. There is a shunting pole on the loco's buffer-beam and the usual collection of oil drums against the shed wall - it was often a problem getting rid of the empties. Note the turntable and the wagon beyond it. Quite a rural scene on the outskirts of London.

North London '2F' 0-6-0T No 58857, Poplar, 3.17 pm, 5.5.56
This was a lucky find during a railtour of the London area, especially since I missed the train which started from Broad Street and had to catch a bus to Poplar to join it. As in many parts of the country, it was possible to see locos of the original company still at work. London docks were then very busy and there were large numbers of local trip trains serving them. Note the target number on the buffer-beam and the ordinary three-link coupling. The tall chimney and dome, capacious cab and outside cylinders were all pleasant attributes of these locos. In addition to this, their home territory, they could be found as far away as Birkenhead and the Peak District.

'61xx' 2-6-2T No 6169, Royal Oak, 9.15 am, 31.7.58, 8.45 am Windsor-Paddington
And so to the Great Western. You can still stand on this platform, but you will only see Hammersmith & City tube trains alongside. The tank engine is very clean and is working a through train from Windsor - nowadays one has to change at Slough. A passenger on the platform is sitting on what appears to be a pigeon hamper - something else that is no longer seen at Royal Oak. Standing on the right are some wagons near the large goods depot adjacent to Paddington station, now completely gone and under redevelopment. The Great Western main line out of Paddington is on the left. The siding next to the loco has inner rails of unusual design.

'Castle' 4-6-0 No 5078 *Beaufort*, Taunton, 1.14 pm, 15.4.54, 11.0 am Paddington-Plymouth
This was a class which attracted a great deal of admiration even from enthusiasts not addicted to the ways of the Great Western. As a native of Leeds, the nearest places where I could observe GW locos were Crewe or Birkenhead, so it was quite an adventure to go on holiday to the heart of the GWR in Somerset. They managed to keep these locos clean even when, elsewhere, most were dirty - and note the GW chocolate and cream coaches. The system of using reporting numbers on the front of locos was common here long before other railways took up the practice; note also that the front coupling on the loco is neatly stowed. The centre platform is not now used, but the rest of the station has not changed much.

'22xx' 0-6-0 No 2244, Cheddar, 5.10 pm, 1.5.62
The orchard and rolling countryside in the background indicate a very pleasant rural area - unfortunately today there are no signs of railway activity. Most of the traffic in this view is on Engineers' business - sleepers, spoil and new ballast. Other items of note are the spare lamp on the running plate of the engine, the large coal hopper wagons near the goods shed and the back of a GW signal on the left. Cheddar station with its all-over roof and signal box are in the distance.

'57xx' 0-6-0T No 9670, Creech St Michael, 1.14 pm, 29.6.60
This is just the type of local freight you expected to see almost anywhere in the West Country; note the bucket and long shovel on the loco's bunker. The GW signals on many parts of the Western main line were still in use until recently; indeed, some were erected in the 1970s on parts of the system. Passengers wishing to cross the line are advised to use the steps and road bridge; there are two signs to this effect, one nearly hidden by the abundant bushes. On the right, a feature of many GW stations, is a tall post with a pulley arrangement for a lamp which could be lowered for filling, trimming, etc.

'45xx' 2-6-2T No 5557, Liskeard, 4.41 pm, 30.6.60

China clay is a type of traffic still very much with us, albeit in more modern wagons, although the change only took effect a few years ago. The old 'Clayhoods' were an archaic survival, and the name Clayliner rather flattered the set of wooden wagons which ran to Stoke with clay for the Potteries. Driver and porter are having a chat whilst guard and shunter (with pole) look ready for action.

The signalman hasn't had a long pull as the points and 'dolly' (ground disc signal) are right outside the box; note that it is the top dolly which is off, indicating a route setting to the left on to the Looe branch. No doubt the engine and van are going down to Moorswater which is behind and to the left of this view, ie the long curve of the Looe branch takes the line round and under the main line. There are barrows loaded with holiday luggage and the fine GW signals are a pleasing feature.

'1400' 0-4-2T No 1466, Tiverton, 11.52 am, 1.5.62

As I write this I can see a Hornby Dublo model of engine No 1466 sitting on the mantlepiece - it is a pity that the full-size version can no longer be found shunting at Tiverton. In May 1962 she was doing this work between trips with the push-and-pull to Tiverton Junction. Sister engine No 1470 was working the Hemyock branch that morning. The shunter is striding along the train with his shunting pole and has just passed under the loading gauge at the exit from the warehouse. In the foreground is a single-line tablet catcher complete with net and a lamp on a separate post directed at the arm of the catcher. Although Tiverton and its junction have lost their stations, there is, of course, a Parkway station now on the main line.

'3MT' 2-6-2T No 82011, Bude, 11.47 am, 30.6.60

Not far away were the West Country lines of the former Southern Railway, the so-called 'Withered Arm'. You could say that one of the reasons for the demise of this line is in the picture. There are five members of staff within sight plus, no doubt, others, including platelayers, not in view. The guard has propped his shunting pole against his SR brake van, a parcels van sits by the bay platform, and seaside hotels overlook the bay. There is a decidedly 'Southern' look about the whole scene, even though we are 229 miles from Waterloo. Note the white disc on the loco smokebox denoting the class of train, and the coaching stock with the number 199 shown on the end.

'2MT' 2-6-2T No 41314, Barnstaple Junction, 9.22 am, 30.6.60
A summer morning at a station which still exists but is now at the end of a branch. Then it was an active part of the ex-LSW routes in the West Country. Behind me and to the left ran the line to Ilfracombe, crossing the estuary of the Taw on a long curving viaduct. Turning off to the right, behind, was the Torrington line, which still carried a portion of the 'Atlantic Coast Express'. The Ivatt Class '2' tanks had recently replaced the ex-LSW 'M7s' on most trains in the area. Note the Bulleid 'light Pacific' being steamed up at the shed in the background, and the odd-looking water column in the right foreground.

'M7' 0-4-4T No 30109, North Camp, 5.41 pm, 13.5.57, 5.5 pm Reading South-Guildford
Here is a pleasant, almost Victorian, scene, back in the ex-SR heartland. In addition to the lovely old 'M7', in very clean condition, the main item is the marvellous 'birdcage' set. This was the way to travel, and certainly a far cry from the Gatwick DMUs which rush along here now. The point about the birdcage roof, at each end of the train, was that the guard could observe the safe working of the train whilst in motion. Even some early BR stock had a system of mirrors for the same purpose, but these were soon given up because they became blackened by smoke. I remember climbing up inside a birdcage at Martin Mill in a set stabled there near a Camping Coach in which we were staying. It was like stepping back into a previous age. At the same station the signal levers were in the booking office! On the platform at North Camp are gas lamps, and the signals are off for another train. In the distance the level crossing gates are closed to road traffic until both trains have passed and the signal is returned to the 'on' position to provide protection.

'M7' 0-4-4T No 30110, Bordon, 7.18 pm, 15.5.57, 7.39 pm to Bentley
It was very pleasant to travel on a branch line like this on a spring evening, but there were very few passengers about - as you can see from this photo, there is nobody in sight. In 1961 I travelled on a train from Eyemouth to Burnmouth in Northumberland on a November evening. There were no other passengers and the signalman at Burnmouth rushed out to light some Tilley lamps for the platform as, for once, he had a passenger!

No 30110 is working in push-and-pull mode, connecting with the Alton electrics at Bentley. Bordon station served an important military area in which was also located the Longmoor Military Railway.

'King Arthur' 4-6-0 No 30765 *Sir Gareth*, Woking, 1.15 pm, 5.7.60, Up freight
Moving nearer London, we have some examples of SR freight, but the first features a sort of loco you would not expect. The 'King Arthurs' were regulars on Salisbury semi-fast trains at the time. The long train seems to consist mainly of 16-ton wagons returning empty to the collieries. I wonder if the schoolboys awaiting their buses on the road beyond the platform wall are still interested in trains. If so, they were probably keen on the more recent Class '50s', and will be impressed, as I am, by the Wessex electrics. The concrete posts, wall and footbridge are normal features of the area.

LSWR '700' Class 0-6-0 No 30689, Weybridge, 3.10 pm, 5.7.60
The vast expanse of LSW main line in the foreground leaves the Class '700' unmoved. The little goods shed with open door and crane outside on the platform are straight out of a Hornby Dublo catalogue. From the cab the driver is looking out as he propels the wagons, but I don't know what the man on the right is doing. Note the LSW chimney and classification discs on the loco, and the rather quaint 'dolly' signal to the front of the buffer-beam. Altogether the sort of scene that bored commuters might like to see today.

'S15' 4-6-0 No 30508, Winchfield, 4.36 pm, 4.7.60, Down freight
Here is the LSW main line before it was transformed by third rail electrification. There are several sidings, as at most stations then, but they appear to be grass grown and little used. The 'S15' has quite a long train with several containers helping to form a 'fitted head' at the front. Later, in the 1970s, the Southern became the first region to go fully fitted, and this caused not a few problems in the days before almost complete transformation to air brakes on BR freight. It meant that other regions had to be careful not to send unfitted wagons to the SR, at a time when they could run elsewhere. In addition, there was the problem of some fitted wagons having vacuum and some air brakes. In some ways we have similar problems nowadays when, although nearly all wagons are air braked, some cannot run at the required speeds. Note the lattice-work signals and lower quadrants in the distance. This is now a London commuter area with frequent electric services.

5
Bramley
April 1959 to November 1960

Bramley was a smoke-blackened station on the Leeds Central to Bradford Exchange line with quite a frequent service using the early BR DMUs; most travelled via the Pudsey branch, now disappeared. There was a small goods yard with a weighbridge which the booking clerk had to operate, and there was even work in helping to unload vans of rags received for the local shoddy mills. A small hand-cranked crane was used for unloading the occasional wagons of steel. One unusual feature of the freight operation at Bramley was the method used to service a private siding at the west end of the yard. Turner's Machinery received a wagon of foundry coke about once a week. A winch, secured to a concrete stopblock, was used to haul the wagon for the last 30 yards or so up a slight incline and round a corner, as the usual 'J39' or 'J6' was not allowed into the siding. Of course the inevitable happened one day! The BR trip engine propelled a wagon into the siding, and the hook of the winch was attached to the drawbar of the wagon before it came to a stand. Result - wagon continues forward, stops, then runs back down hill, taking up slack of rope, winch pulled out of concrete block! From then onwards it was necessary to use a long raft of empty wagons with the coke wagon at the leading end.

Another strange item was a bridge which was officially a bridge when going through in one direction but a tunnel in the other. This was due to a road above crossing the line at an angle.

I heard many tales of other incidents at Bramley and it seems to have been a rather accident prone place, or maybe it was a particular Station Master. Certainly his name was associated with most of the stories.

Coaching stock was often stabled at Bramley in the winter for use on Summer extras, as happened at many stations. One day a couple of coaches had to be detached. The Station Master decided to supervise the operation and assured the guard that, after uncoupling the coaches concerned, it wasn't necessary to do the same with the vacuum pipes - he'd seen it done before. Unfortunately, this time it didn't work! When the driver was given the hand-signal to move forward, out came the pipes, vacuum cylinders and other gear from under the coach.

On another occasion it was the signalman who was out of luck. Again some stabled coaches had to be moved. The siding was guarded by an ancient GN somersault signal, little used of course, so a very strong pull on the lever was necessary. A bit too strong on this occasion - as down came signal, post and all.

Both these stories are railway legends, and I have heard similar ones elsewhere. I am sure they are true of Bramley, even if subject to a little embellishment.

It's nice to read about railway families where several generations have served the railway over long periods. However, there have been and, no doubt, still are people who make a great impression during a short time on the railway scene. One such was Jack Cornwell, who was a porter at Bramley during my time there as a booking clerk. The other porter was Mrs Jean Parker who lived in the station house, above the booking office.

Jack's main claim to fame was that he played his violin to entertain the passengers. This was a great boon if the train was late - or even if it wasn't - as his wit was enjoyed by the passengers along with the fiddling. He used to boast that he had started work in 1910 on the LSWR at Haslemere. In those days he had to line up each morning with the other porters for inspection by the Station Master. Corduroy trousers were part of the uniform and, if you were not neat and tidy and clean shaven, you were sent home with the loss of a day's pay. What Jack didn't tell you, until pressed, was that he left after three weeks to join the Marines! He served throughout the First

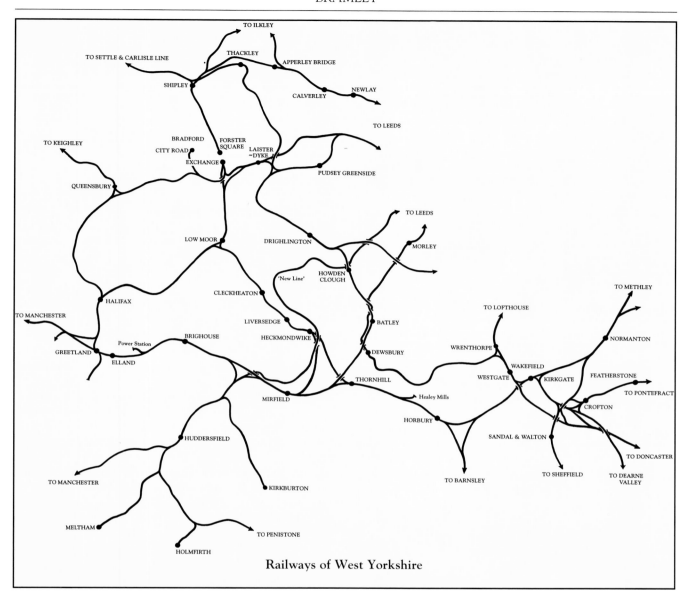

Railways of West Yorkshire

World War, including a trip to Archangel to assist the White Russians. A page from history indeed, and now a second Revolution is taking place in that far-off land.

Jack was always keen on music and earned a living in the 1920s playing in theatre orchestras, mainly Music Hall. Here he met his wife, who appeared on the stage. Eventually Jack achieved his ambition - to lead his own ensemble. This took him to Yorkshire where many large hotels had their own trios or quartets in the 1930s. War came again and Jack joined Leeds City Tramways. Soon he was conductor of the band and was made Inspector. In the 1950s came ill health. He admitted that he joined BR mainly to have an incentive to get out of the house each day and keep moving rather than become an invalid. It is amazing to think now of the number of people in

their 50s who were taken on in those days of full employment. I knew several.

One of Jack's favourite tricks was to do an impression of an old-time cabbie. He would sit on a chair back with his BR mac placed loosely around his shoulders, his top hat down over his nose and his yardstick in his hand acting as a whip. (This stick was a piece of wood a yard long. Jack had read a letter from District Office - one of the advantages of being on early turn when the letters arrived! - saying that something or other should be used as a 'yardstick', so he decided he would have one!)

One of Jack's main aversions was pigeons. Most of the pigeon traffic was, of course, in train-loads to places like Berwick for long races. There were, however, training flights, and we sent quite a few baskets to Ardsley or other local stations early in the pigeon season and received some, similarly, for release for short trips. The empty baskets had to be returned with the label endorsed with the time of release of the birds. Jack hated these noisy and noisome creatures and would put the wrong times on the labels to create confusion. He also had a scheme to train groups of birds to carry their own baskets back home, but somehow this idea didn't quite 'take off'!

He got into a bit of trouble when he decided to paint all the platform lamp-posts red, and was soon told to restore them to their original green. A District Office man had observed them from the train and reported the matter. His final trick, which he also failed to get away with, was to get the SM to enter for the Station Garden Competition. To achieve quick results, Jack buried some potted plants in the garden. Unfortunately it rained heavily the night before the inspection by the big-wigs from District Office, revealing the pots! Needless to say we didn't win a prize. The date of the inspection was always, of course, kept secret to prevent any such tricks.

Jack was a marvellous character and a true railwayman, even though he was on BR for only a short while. He served the public and brought a smile to many a face on a cold morning.

I spent every third Saturday afternoon in Bramley box learning block signalling. Vince, the signalman, was very happy to relax in the old armchair, a regular feature in most boxes. The signalman at Armley Moor always knew I was there as he recognised the different speed at which I tapped out the telegraph bell signals compared with Vince. Each bell also had its own tone so that you knew which was ringing. This was also a regular arrangement and very necessary with four tracks and a junction, even if the goods lines were little used.

The booking office was lit by gas which made it rather unpleasant at times - hot on summer evenings, and the air difficult to breathe in winter when the lamps were, of course, on for longer periods. In addition, the mantles were difficult to obtain as not many people still used them. The smell when you 'burned

in' a new one was quite unforgettable, but it was necessary.

The tickets were all of the Edmondson card type with pillar date stamper; it was a skilled job, last thing at night, to change the metal date numbers without dropping them all over the floor.

Parcels traffic was quite heavy, and two types were rather unusual. One firm made shampoo and dispatched cartons containing the bottles to hairdressers in local towns. The cartons were open at the top so that nobody could be in doubt as to their damageable contents. Strange to relate, few thefts of the bottles took place. Another firm sent small metal castings, painted blue. Unfortunately the painting was done at the last minute before they were brought to the station; the result was that local railwaymen went around with blue hands, demanding turpentine!

The parcels trains were usually worked by Stanier Class '3' tanks or GN 'J6s'. One evening a Stanier marginally passed a signal at danger in the dark. The signalman knew, of course, because it showed up on his track diagram above the frame. The driver also knew and asked me to convey his apologies, which were accepted. This was on one of the many occasions when I was on duty until after the last train at 11 pm, covering for a porter. The last job was to turn off all the gas lamps after removing the ashes from the fireplaces in the booking office and waiting room.

The Station Master at the time wasn't very popular on one occasion when a Stanier Class '4' tank seized up on the main line. After a lot of delay he decided not to put in single line working but to convey the schoolchildren from Armley Moor to Bramley in a DMU on the goods line. The trouble was that there were no platforms at either station on the goods line!

Both stations have since been demolished but Bramley was re-opened a few years ago, unstaffed of course and with just a shelter on each platform. These are somewhat staggered as at the original station. However, it is nice to know that there is now a considerably better service than ever before.

'4MT' 2-6-4T No 42311, Bramley, 3.41 pm, 8.9.60, 1.10 pm Southport-Leeds Central

Bramley in all its glory, complete with flowers painted on the concrete shelter on the left-hand platform! Note also the water crane and distant signal box on the left. The stock is, of course, LMS, and the Fowler tank is approaching the wooden foot crossing used by the porter. The station coal was unloaded, sometimes by me, from a wagon placed behind the waiting room on the right. The arrival of station or signal box coal was always a big event and caused a lot of problems if not ordered in time or delayed *en route*. Note the three fire buckets near the waiting room. These were supposed to contain water or, during freezing weather, sand.

After many years' absence the right-hand platform has been reopened with a new structure; the other one is now behind the photographer at the far side of a road bridge.

'Patriot' 4-6-0 No 45539 *E. C. Trench*, Bramley, 9.5 am, 2.6.60, 8.17 am Sowerby Bridge-Leeds Central
This was an unusual sort of train and produced a wide variety of locos. All the trains that called at Bramley were DMUs; indeed, this was the first line to have BR diesel units. You could say that they were running what used to be the local GN service. Trains passing through Bramley were mainly a perpetuation of the old L&Y service, which consisted of portions from Leeds Central and Bradford Exchange which joined at Low Moor before continuing over the Pennines to Liverpool Exchange. The train in the photo was a morning rush-hour addition and, like the Leeds portions, avoided Bradford by means of the Laisterdyke-Bowling cut-off, now disappeared. There were other places in the 1960s where a similar pre-Grouping situation prevailed.
  Note the box of fish near the edge of the platform awaiting delivery to a local works canteen in time for lunch. The station garden is on the right. On the left, the platform was a source of trouble if a DMU stopped a bit short in the dark - more than one late-night reveller ended up in the cess but not, fortunately, over the fence on to the road below.

'Crab' 2-6-0 No 42863, Howden Clough, 6.46 pm, 22.7.61, 12.20 pm (SO) Yarmouth-Bradford Exchange
The 'Crab' is making light work of its train on the steep gradient. Howden Clough box was an attractive structure lacking only a coat of paint, which it probably did not get as the line did not survive for much longer. The pointwork on the left is interesting - because of the lack of space, two sets of traps had to be fitted into a small area. A sort distance away another line, long disappeared, crossed underneath; this was the 'New Line' from Farnley Junction to Huddersfield via the Spen Valley. At the time it still served one of its original purposes - to keep traffic clear of the congested route via Dewsbury and Mirfield. Its other purpose, to serve the Spen Valley towns, had ceased. The other Spen line, from Bradford to Mirfield, was still open at this time. The line illustrated was one of three between Wakefield and Bradford and provided the woollen towns of Dewsbury, Batley and Ossett with a local as well as a through London service.

'J39' 0-6-0 No 64705, Adolphus Street, 4.45 pm, 5.9.61
Here is a very industrial scene on the steeply graded line out of Bradford. The train probably originated on the Queensbury line and would be going to Laisterdyke. Note the wooden coal wagon conveying scrap; this is of the swarf variety, ie waste metal from machining or turning processes, rather than the more commonly known scrap in the form of cut-up cars, etc. On the left is Adolphus Street, one of the large Bradford goods stations, and the scene, at about this time, of a runaway 'L1' tank which careered through the depot; it was a type new to the area which probably explains the incident. On the right was Hammerton Street DMU depot, previously the GN loco shed.

'B1' 4-6-0 No 61129, Armley Moor, 2.35 pm, 31.12.61, 1.20 pm (Suns) Harrogate-King's Cross
You need to be a bit of a detective to discover why most of this train has snow on the roof but not all. The reason is that the rear coaches have come through from Harrogate and have been attached to the Leeds portion at Central station. The Leeds coaches must have had very good insulation, or perhaps the heat just hasn't percolated through yet. I once travelled on an early train from Leeds to Darlington on a similar day; 90 minutes later, on arrival at Darlington, the train was still frozen both inside and out. On the next day we had a brand new High Speed Train - sheer bliss!

Armley box is switched out even though the line is being used for diverted London trains. The lamp room for the oil signal lamps is on the left; a full-time lampman was based here, covering Bramley as well. Small GN signals control the sidings where many coaches and wagons are standing. The blackened stone buildings disappeared after the station was closed in 1966, although there are plans for its re-opening.

'Black Five' 4-6-0 No 44990, Low Moor, 2.19 pm, 30.3.58, 1.48 pm (Suns) Leeds Central and 2.7 pm Bradford Exchange-Liverpool Exchange
This was the station where the two portions of the Liverpool trains were attached and detached. Note the extensive facilities provided - General Room, Ladies Room, substantial roof over both platforms and the gas lamps. The L&Y signals, glimpsed above the signal box roof, were becoming something of a rarity, to the east of the Pennines anyway. The box is No 2 West, indicating the extent of the signalling in the area and the L&Y practice of numbering its boxes. The 'Black Five' is on its home ground and is blowing off ready for departure. We tend to forget the annoyance this caused to passengers, but it was accepted by enthusiasts in the same way, perhaps, as the noise of a departing HST nowadays. The LMS stock prevailed until dieselisation three years later.

'Patriot' 4-6-0 No 45517, Bradford Exchange, 5.7 pm, 5.9.61
This very depressing panorama for anyone unaccustomed to the area is enlivened somewhat by the 'Patriot' which is propelling its empty stock out of Exchange station. These were fine-looking locos but not very common on the Liverpool trains. It was also strange to have a class of locos some of which were named and some not - No 45517 drew a short straw and spent its life anonymously.

For many years there were two distinct halves to Exchange - L&Y and GN. The old station has now gone completely and has been replaced by a new one, with good interchange facilities, next to a large bus station. There is today a lively, well-used local service hereabouts, with frequent trains to Leeds, Halifax and Manchester.

'4F' 0-6-0 No 44062, Armley Moor, 2.27 pm, 18.6.60, 11.30 am Liverpool Exchange-Leeds Central
It always seemed rather strange to see '4Fs' on passenger trains, particularly carrying Class 1 lamps, but quite a few could be seen on branch trains. This train is running between stations both of which have now gone although there is an intensive local service on this route. The goods lines, on the left, were not used a great deal and have now been lifted. The loco is coasting down towards Leeds with coupling rods spinning - there are no more stops as Holbeck High Level had now closed. In 1958 I saw a similar train, also with Class 1 lamps, but the loco was an incredibly ancient L&Y 0-6-0 pressed into service on a Summer Saturday, perhaps for the very last time.

'3MT' 2-6-2T No 40148, Hunslet, 6.25 pm, 7.5.60, 6.20 pm Leeds City-Cudworth
I was trying out my newly acquired Leica camera on this May evening over 30 years ago. Beeching was yet to come but this station closed even before the famous cuts began. At the time it seemed that inner city stations like these had no future, being located in more of an industrial than a residential area. In May 1960 it was still manned and I was able to purchase an Edmondson card ticket as a souvenir. Nowadays this type of station might survive, but unmanned. It is on the Midland main line with the busy goods lines running behind the platforms. Holbeck shed is out of sight beyond the station buildings. The loco is the large-boilered version of the rather attractive Stanier Class '3' tank class.

'Black Five' 'Caprotti' 4-6-0 No 44744, Bramley, 5.20 pm, 20.6.60, 5.10 pm Leeds Central-Liverpool Exchange
The 5.10 pm was one exception to the rule that Liverpool trains had a tank engine from Leeds to Low Moor. The loco for this train ran light, tender first, presumably from Low Moor shed, and was very often a Bank Hall 'Caprotti' - I used to leave the booking office for a few minutes to see it go through. Such a light load was no problem for this type, even on the steep gradients in the Holbeck area. In the goods yard, to the left, can be seen a van containing rags for a local mill, and several coal trucks. As usual there is a set of stabled coaching stock on the right, with a GN 'somersault' signal controlling the exit from the siding.

'B1' 4-6-0 No 61017 *Bushbuck*, Howden Clough, 1.43 pm, 3.4.61, 11.55 am Goole-Bradford Exchange
DMUs had by this time taken over many of the local services but it is Easter and several steam sets have been diagrammed to replace them for a few days. Hopefully a Goole service via Featherstone will reappear in the future, but it will not use this switchback line via Dewsbury. In my enthusiasm to capture the GN signal as well as the train I picked the wrong spot and so had the signal sticking out of the smokebox! Note that the middle pair of coaches of the set are articulated, sharing a common central bogie.

'J50' 0-6-0T No 68944, Pudsey Lowtown, 10.41 am, 2.6.60, Bramley-Pudsey Greenside Class J
This pleasant summer scene belies an industrial area just out of sight. The shirt-sleeved guard, sitting on the steps of the brake van, is more fortunate than the fireman on this hot day. The sheeted wagon has a longitudinal bar to hold a sheet but, in this case, appears not to be used. When fitted with shock-absorbing equipment, such a wagon would revel in the name of a SHOCHIBARFIT!

On the right is fog signalling equipment - a lever, when pulled, would place a detonator on the line, which would be done if the adjacent distant signal was at caution. The man doing this, invariably a platelayer, had a small wooden hut with provision for a coal fire. He would, of course, bring the detonators with him - they would not be kept in the hut for fear of theft - and the Supervisor had to ensure that they were in good condition and not out of date. Similarly, at a signal box, the Station Master checked the detonators in the device for placing them on the line in case of emergency. Note the contrasting upper and lower quadrant distants worked from different signal boxes - that on the left is the Bramley up branch distant and the other belongs to Lowtown.

'K3' 2-6-0 No 61935, Bradford, 6.4 pm, 15.4.61, 6.0 pm return excursion Bradford Exchange-Hull Paragon
This train was one of many taking rugby enthusiasts home after the match at Odsal stadium. In those days there was no need to separate the supporters by using different stations. Even now there is far less trouble from rugby compared with soccer fans. Exchange station was used for purely logistical reasons to assist in moving large numbers of people in a short space of time. There was also more than a touch of pre-nationalisation working about it too. Hull was more easily reached using ex-GN and NE lines from Exchange. Note the mainly BR Mark I stock in use, then quite new. Broomfield sidings, on the right, served Exchange station. The line going underneath originally went to Halifax GN and Keighley GN, but the passenger service disappeared in 1955, although the line continued in use for freight including a link to City Road goods. There are more, extensive, sidings on the left at Springmill Street, which included coal drops. Note the banking engine in use at the rear because of the heavy gradient - this was not a normal feature of the line as most trains were not heavy enough to need assistance.

'Jubilee' 4-6-0 No 45688 _Polyphemus_, Low Moor, 5.7 pm, 15.4.61, 5.6 pm return excursion Low Moor-St Helens
This is another excursion taking rugby enthusiasts home after the match at Odsal stadium, which was a fair walk up the hill from Low Moor.

This was an area of considerable activity at the time; now there is virtually nothing left. To a certain extent this was because, like a number of other places on BR, it was essentially an operating rather than a commercial centre. The station was busy because L&Y trains were divided or joined there; however, it didn't serve a large local community and was later closed. There was also a fair-sized engine shed at Low Moor which became even busier when Bradford GN shed closed, with consequent transfer of locos. The large carriage sidings and rakes of mainly ex-LMS screw-coupled coaches were typical of the period. Stock was held all the year round to provide sets for the busy periods - Bank Holidays, Wakes Weeks and, of course, the Rugby League Cup Final at Wembley. At Distribution of Coaching Stock Offices in Leeds we received a hand-written stock sheet daily. During the winter it hardly changed, but somebody still went round each day to record all the numbers. Across the back of the carriage sidings ran the Spen Valley line to Cleckheckmondsedge.

6
Trains Office, Leeds
November 1960-December 1961

My first promotion came at the age of 22 and I was told how lucky I was to be a Class 3 clerk at such an early age; most of the bosses had been around since before the war when promotion prospects were grim. This year or so in District Office was useful experience, but convinced me that my career lay outside rather than at a desk for eight hours a day.

In 1960 there was a vast quantity of steam-hauled coaching stock around; a large proportion in my area was of LNER or LMS origin. There was not much involved in the day-to-day running as the stock was mainly on planned diagrams worked out to fit the timetable, or possibly vice versa - I was not around long enough to find out which was true! There was regular strengthening, ie adding extra coaches to trains, especially at weekends and holidays; this is something nearly unheard of nowadays.

Horseboxes and Special Cattle Vans were dealt with and, like everything else, this meant sending out large numbers of internal telegrams to yards, Control Offices, Station Masters, etc. The telegrams were known as wires and they were written out on special forms ready for the office messenger to take to the Telegraph Office. If you needed to send external Post Office telegrams they were free of charge in recognition of the fact that the wires over which they were sent were alongside BR tracks. What happened to all those telegraph poles? They don't seem to be around nowadays.

Other special movements were 'wired out' and I nearly came to grief with one of these. In the summer of 1961 a school at Featherstone was going camping. There was no parcels train on that line and I was given the job of arranging for a 'vanfit' containing the gear to be picked up by a Hull-Mirfield freight one evening. The idea was for a transfer to take place at Mirfield for onward transit by passenger train to Portmadoc where Jones the Post (yes, that was his accepted name!) would arrange the unloading before

the children arrived on Saturday morning. Unfortunately my wad of wires to be sent out did not include one for the Yard Master at Mirfield, so the inevitable happened. Luckily for me, Jones the Post took his duties very seriously and soon kicked up a fuss when the van failed to arrive on time. After a sleepless night for me, the van was tracked down at Mold Junction, having arrived there on a freight train from Mirfield. A special pilot rushed the van to Chester General and it arrived at Portmadoc in the nick of time. Relief all round!

This incident serves to illustrate a bygone era, as does the question of 'guaranteed excursions'; these GAREXs were mainly for Miners clubs and invariably included a parcels van in the middle to act as the bar. Most ran on Sundays in June and July; Saturdays and August were out of the question as all the stock would be in use elsewhere. As it was, most of the coaches for this type of traffic stood around all winter doing nothing, so all winter we made up files with the details of these and liaised with Regional HQ to ensure that there would be enough stock of the required types.

There were many movements of empty stock between the numerous carriage sidings in the West Riding; all had to be wired out and it was easy from our point of view. However, of course, each move involved somebody finding a loco and a train crew who knew the road. On several occasions at peak weekends we had to book a whole train back empty from King's Cross in order to work another up train later in the day. A traditional trick was to ensure that such a set was of the LMS screw-coupled type as King's Cross would not be tempted to hang on to these - all their stock was LNER or BR buckeye.

Light relief away from the office was provided by a member of the staff who had an arrangement with the Refreshment Room manager at Leeds City to provide casual staff - we were all roped in at one time or another. I also had two trips to Paignton. The train was from Bradford Forster Square but we boarded at Leeds at 9.15 pm on a Summer Friday. Arrival at Paignton was usually an hour late on these trips due to the heavy traffic, even early on Saturday morning. On the outward trip we made tea in a large urn in our reserved compartment, then at Bristol, at about 3 am, we re-brewed. Some people sat up all night and had a standing order for tea on the hour, every hour. Others spread themselves out and slept - there was normally room for them to do so. A quick breakfast was taken at Paignton, then we returned on the 8.50 am which was a reserved train and always full. Many were the black looks when people saw our two reserved compartments which they thought was reducing the number of seats available but, of course, it was allowed for. Anyway, the same people were soon glad of our services on the long journey back to the North. At about 2 shillings (10p) an hour we were hardly overpaid, but around 21 hours continuous duty multiplied by 2 bob added up to a reasonable amount.

On my second trip, behind a 'Jubilee' after the mandatory loco change at Bristol where ex-GW handed over to ex-LMS, we used the Gloucester bypass line. We then converged, rather rapidly, alongside a 'Black Five'-hauled train getting away from its Gloucester stop. This event took place at Barnwood and, after some alarm on the part of the passengers, we settled down to a fine race along the quadruple track towards Cheltenham. At one stage the cab of the 'Black Five' was opposite our compartment and, as it was on the adjacent line, I was able to pass over a carton of orange squash to the exhausted fireman. The effect was dramatic! His train immediately pulled ahead with every coach slowly passing us. By this time the passengers on both trains were entering into the spirit of the race, with loud cheers on the other train turning to groans as we were 'given the road' into Lansdown station and the 'Black Five' ground to a halt, with a final wave from the sporting train crew. Of such events are railway legends made - would that it were possible now. On the same stretch I have been on trains well beaten by marvellous little '1400' Class 0-4-2 tanks with one-coach push-and-pulls. Well, they were on their home ground and certainly not overawed by large LMS types!

But to return to earth again and the Trains Office.

It served the Wakefield District and was set up to look after the so-called 'penetrating lines' after nationalisation. This was a rather untidy business whereby the District was to look after all ex-GN and L&Y lines which crossed the NE Region boundary. These lines not only intertwined with the former NE, LNW and Midland lines which constituted the Leeds District, but there were also other problems. Whereas Leeds had its obvious centre at City station, with a thriving Control and other offices in the pre-war LMS offices, Wakefield had no natural centre. The L&Y was naturally inclined towards Manchester, even at this late stage, and the GN had a small Control at Leeds Central which I once visited as a schoolfriend's father was a Station Foreman there. When I arrived on the scene there was a Control at Wakefield Westgate and the Trains Office had just moved from Central to City station in Leeds. The Chief Clerk was in a fortunate position often sought by many people, ie he was always at the *other* office when needed at Leeds or Wakefield.

Cleaning arrangements were part of the routine of the job and we had Inspectors who went round to check on this. These men were passed out in 'Rules and Regs' so they could stand in for a guard or 'conduct' one as I often did in later years - if a driver or guard was unfamiliar with a particular line and had not 'signed for the road', it was necessary to provide a local man to conduct him. This system is quite well known so far as drivers were concerned but perhaps not so in respect of guards. When I was Assistant Area Manager at Knottingley I conducted many guards and even the occasional driver, which was certainly unusual.

There was trouble one Easter when a train of 'block-enders' (non-corridor stock) was turned out to work an excursion after being stabled all winter. The steam heating had to be turned on as it was very cold and the effect was quite dramatic - the passengers refused to get into the musty, steamy compartments and another set had to be hastily provided. In those days you could usually find something fairly quickly.

The type of work I was doing was set to decline quite rapidly as the accelerating DMU schemes came into operation and Beeching decided that stock should not be kept all year just to work half a dozen trips in the summer. This was my only experience of working in a District or Divisional Office, as it was to become. Both sorts have now disappeared into the history of BR activities.

'A1' 4-6-2 No 60130 *Kestrel*, Whitehall Junction, 5.14 pm, 10.8.63

One of the advantages of working on the distribution of coaching stock was that you knew about this type of regular movement. A King's Cross to Leeds train, on arrival at Central station, had most of its stock removed by a pilot. The three coaches next to the engine were, however, left, and the main-line loco which had worked from King's Cross then propelled them to Holbeck Low Level and thence to Neville Hill. *Kestrel* has just gone through Low Level, half way between Central and City stations. The signalman on the left, although only controlling one corner of a triangle, still has a considerable number of points and signals to deal with.

'V2' 2-6-2 No 60872 *King's Own Yorkshire Light Infantry*, Leeds Central, 3.8 pm, 12.8.61, 10.20 am King's Cross-Leeds

The marshalling of this train is rather odd. A full BG parcels van seems excessive on a busy Summer Saturday train, and the buffet car then comes next. Bearing in mind that the Bradford portion was at the rear of the train as far as Wakefield, this meant quite a walk for passengers using the latter. The named 'V2' looks to be in fine condition. This sort of train might have had any type of 'Pacific' - 'A1', 'A2','A3' or 'A4' - but 'V2s' were also quite common. The L&Y/LNW part of Wellington Street goods is on the right. Many years previously it was common to see a 'C12' tank engine arrive on a local and then propel the empty stock out of the station. The loco would then be detached and the coaches gravitated back into the station under the control of the guard or shunter.

'O2' 2-8-0 No 63936, Stainforth & Hatfield, 2.52 pm, 7.5.63

I considered these to be fine locos, not least because they continued to carry out heavy duties well into the 1960s despite their ancient GN lineage. Stainforth was a busy yard, lying as it did near Scunthorpe and several collieries and power stations. Beyond the engine is a plate wagon - there were thousands of these in use for steel plate and, even now, the air-braked equivalent performs a similar service. During the building of the new yard at Scunthorpe nearly all traffic was held at Stainforth yard before being called forward to go to the various parts of the BSC complex. One result of this was that block trains of coal from Grimethorpe were worked as follows: Grimethorpe-Carlton-Wath-Hexthorpe-Stainforth-Scunthorpe. Each was a separate movement with a different loco and train crew, each leg getting the train a bit nearer its destination.

'A1' 4-6-2 No 60135 *Madge Wildfire*, Naburn, 3.55 pm, 23.4.62, Up Parcels

Madge Wildfire has just crossed the River Ouse and is heading along a unique line - that part of the ECML now replaced by the new line, the Selby Diversion, between Temple Hirst and Colton. It is interesting that the parcels train also conveys an LNER coach and a modern Pullman car. The fine lattice-posted lower quadrant signals, closed station buildings and NE goods yard complete the picture, but this locality no longer sees a constant procession of trains on a line so busy for so many years.

'Jubilee' 4-6-0 No 45622 *Nyasaland*, Chinley, 12.1 pm, 25.6.60, Down 'Palatine'
The 'Palatine' was important enough to justify the latest BR Mark I stock in 1960, although within a few years both it and the St Pancras to Manchester service generally, together with the Peak District line between Matlock and Buxton, would be gone. The sheer scale of buildings, platforms, track and pointwork, signals and bridges is amazing when you compare it with what remains today - just one island platform, shelter and short footbridge. There is not a trace of smoke or steam as the 'Jubilee' coasts down the hill after the earlier hard work, climbing the Pennines on a hot Summer Saturday.

'Jubilee' 4-6-0 No 45651 *Showell*, Chinley, 12.51 pm, 25.6.60, 11.40 am Manchester Central-Chinley
Another 'Jubilee' is coming the other way, the delightfully named *Showell*. At the age of about 12 such a name often featured in our trainspotter competitions - for example, what happens when a man goes on to a building site? Answer: *E. C. Trench* ('Patriot' Class). Or what county is in the West Country? *Cornwallis* ('Jubilee' Class)! *Showell* has a light load of non-corridor stock more suited to the rush hour than a Saturday local. The driver has shut off for the run in to the Chinley stop. All is quiet, for the time being, on the fast lines. Now the ubiquitous DMU covers this type of job.

'4F' 0-6-0 No 43844, Hellifield, 10.58 am, 6.8.60, 7.48 am (SO) Sheffield Midland-Morecambe
This '4F' is making a fine show in very pleasant country scenery - plenty of steam and effort. As usual on a Summer Saturday, everything is out on the line. The first three coaches are from a Mark I set, but the train then degenerates into a mixture of old LNER stock. It wasn't unknown for non-corridor stock to be used on Leeds-Morecambe excursions despite the distance and the time taken. This train was one of a procession of Morecambe and Settle & Carlisle trains, mainly hauled by 'Black Fives'. I was actually on my way to Shap but this seemed too good a shot to miss.

'Patriot' 4-6-0 No 45510, Low Gill, 1.35 pm, 6.8.60, Down Class C
I always regarded the 'Patriots' as being very photogenic and with a special character all their own. Perhaps it was the parallel boiler and the pleasing chimney? Anyway, one in good condition was a joy to behold, especially in such a setting. This parcels train is preceding a long run of down expresses. Note the goods brake van and vanfits marshalled in the train - the latter were often used for carrying parcels as well as heavier goods on freight trains. This lovely spot was later to be spoiled by the wires and the M6 motorway.

'4MT' 2-6-4T No 42396, Shap Wells, 3.42 pm, 6.8.60
This oil train is an interesting example of how such trains used to be marshalled. As we are still in the days of steam there are a couple of 16-ton mineral wagons at each end to act as barriers. There is also, of course, a brake van; this is an item nowadays only required for toxic and a few other types of train, not oil traffic. The Fowler tank carries a target number - '93' - and is banking the train up the incline. Such trains managed to find slots even on a busy Saturday. The driver is keeping a good look-out ahead and the leading loco appears to be doing most of the work. Perhaps the banker was partly intended to prevent runaways of unbraked wagons rather than to do a lot of the work.

'WD' 2-8-0 No 90127 and 'B1' 4-6-0 No 61276, Bardsey, 6.8 pm, 3.4.61, 6.0 pm return excursion Wetherby-Heeley

This was the only time I caught a 'WD' on a Class 1 train. It is on the line from Harrogate to Leeds via Wetherby which disappeared many years ago. The races at Wetherby provided many interesting excursions including some double heading due to the severe gradients. The train is of corridor stock as befits its journey to Heeley, in the suburbs of Sheffield. Note the oil-lamp case, cast iron NER trespass notice and LNER station name sign; also to be seen is a 'Stop, Look and Listen' board on the left for the crossing and a long run of point rodding.

'Crab' 2-6-0 No 42795, Farnley & Wortley, 2.43 pm, 18.6.60, Empty stock

During the extensive remodelling of the Leeds area lines due to the rebuilding of City station and the closure of Central, this stretch of line was removed. Previously it had been the main LNW Leeds-Manchester route, but there was a parallel line through Copley Hill yards which is now used. The Leeds-Doncaster line is in the background and a connection was put in so that King's Cross trains could use the LNW viaducts line into Leeds in the distance. Note the bracket signal already back 'on'; beneath it can just be glimpsed a short 'calling on' signal. The bridge just beyond the signals carries a footpath used by generations of supporters on their way to the Leeds United ground nearby. The 'Crab' 2-6-0s were popular locos on this line and could turn their hand to most jobs.

L&Y 'Radial Tank' 2-4-2T No 50850, Southport, 4.15 pm, 29.10.60

It was a long way from Leeds to Southport on a Saturday afternoon in late October after spending the morning in the booking office. There was a good reason for the trip, though - No 50850 was the last of this famous class of L&Y tank engines still at work. She was known to be on station pilot duty, a job now no longer required at this or most other stations. She certainly made a good steam shot and was reasonably clean. Note the ancient Scottish coach, and the firebox iron perched precariously on the side tank.

Returning home in the dark, the journey seemed even longer. 'Crab' No 42722 worked the 4.25 pm all stations to Manchester; following this a 'Black Five' managed to take just over 2 hours all stations to Leeds.

'Britannia' 4-6-2 No 70044 *Earl Haig*, Leeds City, 1.52 pm, 8.3.61, Down 'Waverley'
Earl Haig is making a lot of smoke and blowing off, but the postmen on the right have finished their work so the journey can soon continue to Edinburgh via the S&C and Waverley routes. This train and the 'Thames-Clyde Express' were favourites in the Leeds area for many years. One can still travel all the way from St Pancras to Glasgow via Dumfries, but the Waverley route closed over 20 years ago. In the left background is the 1930s LMS office block which, at that time, housed the Trains Office and, later, the Leeds Divisional Office. Note the spare brake and heater pipes on the platform ready for use, and the tail lamp and short ladder. The objects leaning against the nearer post appear to be gangway boards used to cover the exterior gangway connections at each end of a train.

'V2' 2-6-2 No 60966, Doncaster, 5.1 pm, 25.5.63, Up Parcels
This is a mixed train of parcels vans and empty coaches. The 'V2' has just joined the fast line for the south - the lines to the left sweep round towards Sheffield, and the loco works are in the left background.

'Donny' was always an exciting station to visit. A streamlined 'A4' 'Pacific' approaching at speed on the through lines would set up a cry of 'Streak!' or 'Run through!' from the assembled spotters. The goods yard is busy and there is the usual standby 'Pacific' hidden behind the first line of vans. Now most of this area is electrified and the 'run throughs' go by ever faster and, thankfully, in even greater numbers.

'B1' 4-6-0 No 61235, Sandal, 4.35 pm, 11.3.61, 4.10 pm Leeds Central-Cleethorpes
The once-a-day Cleethorpes service ran for many years and was, at one time, worked by an ex-GC 4-4-0 'Director'. Note the leading pair of coaches, an articulated pre-war set built for the 'Coronation'. It was part of the Cleethorpes train for a long time, but a few months later it was temporarily removed one Saturday at Leeds Central owing to an unfortunate incident. I actually saw someone put his head out of the window in order to find the door handle. Unfortunately the window was closed at the time, so the set had to be replaced while the broken window was repaired. The luckless person, who was just seeing someone off, was also repaired, and I saw him leaving the station with a liberal supply of BR Elastoplasts on his forehead. The 'WD' in the background is propelling its brake van up the Midland main line.

'B16' 4-6-0 No 61447, Crossgates, 11.0 am, 6.6.60, Leeds-Scarborough excursion
This train provides a fine sight even if the loco is very dirty. The residents of this area are no longer subjected to such smoke and neither do day-trippers travel 65 miles in non-corridor stock. The first two vehicles are articulated, ie the middle bogie of the three supports the inner ends of both coaches. This had the advantage of saving weight and maintenance but meant that if one coach was defective both were out of service. Note the chalked reporting number on the smokebox - this was used in the Special Traffic Notices to identify the train to all concerned as being an extra. The points and signals signify that Crossgates was the junction for the Wetherby branch.

'Jubilee' 4-6-0 No 45596 *Bahamas*, Cardigan Road, 1.14 pm, 10.3.64, 11.35 am Neville Hill-Cardigan Road Class 9
It is rather strange to see *Bahamas* on such a job but, at the time, she was just another loco ready to go where required. A lot of changes were taking place in 1964 which resulted in the old order disappearing quite quickly. From a position in the 1950s where pre-Grouping engines still served their old haunts, the last few years of steam brought many odd and, in this case, inappropriate situations. It was nice to see a 'Jubilee' shunting the coal drops, but it was hardly the sort of job for which she was designed. The signal box and coal drops are just beyond the footbridge; the latter was unusual in having a zig-zag slope at the right-hand end.

'Q6' 0-8-0 No 63420, Poole in Wharfedale, 10.33 am, 12.11.63, Class 9 for Neville Hill

What a pity that this goods depot, passenger station and line have now gone. Back in 1963 it was a typical NE depot being served by a 'Q6' trip engine from Neville Hill. Note the wooden NE coal hoppers outside the shed, which bears the hallmarks of a derailment, ie extensive repairs to the stonework. Wooden foot-boarding enables the shunter to pass over the point rodding on the left. Adjacent to the far track, beyond the loco's tender, can be seen a typical heavy NE point lever of the 'throw-over' type, ie its weight ensured a full movement of the point rod so that the switch blade fitted up properly in the normal or reverse positions. Your photographer is standing in someone's allotment garden!

7

East Leake, GC

January 1962-March 1963

This was my first Station Master's job and the happiest. The station lay 9 miles south of Nottingham Victoria on the former Great Central main line and I must admit that I hadn't heard of it when the job appeared on the weekly vacancy list. Although nearly all stations still had Station Masters in those days, the main reason for having one at East Leake was to look after the freight traffic. The passenger work - issuing tickets (Edmundson type) and dealing with parcels - was nothing out of the ordinary except, perhaps, that at Rushcliffe Halt the tickets were booked by the two porters, so I had to do a thorough check each day.

Most of the freight originated at Hotchley Hill sidings adjacent to Rushcliffe Halt and about a mile north of East Leake station. We supplied empty wagons using an Annesley trip which started from Queens Walk, Nottingham, where it collected any empty 'Shocvans' for the plasterboard traffic and empty hoppers returning from Bletchington. At Gotham Sidings the trip then collected 16-tonners left there by an earlier Woodford-Annesley 'Windcutter' which would put off its whole train of empties to keep us going for a few days. These had to have their coal dust swept out on placement at the customer's siding at Hotchley Hill.

The two porters worked alternate early and late turns. One man was a Goods Porter, the other a Porter Signalman. The first few hours were spent issuing tickets and dealing with parcels in the small wooden office at the top of the ramp to the platforms. Then, if the Goods porter was on early, he would stay back, on overtime, to go to the sidings where he dealt with the labelling of the wagons - one label on each side of every wagon - then brought the consignment notes up to the office. He also, of course, assisted with the shunting. If the Porter Signalman was on early turn he would stay on to open Hotchley Hill signal box for a couple of hours for the two trips.

The Annesley engine returned home with the gypsum traffic for the north, mainly for Hope and Penyffordd cement works. The other trip came from Leicester. On its northward run it conveyed Ministry of Defence road vehicles for auction at Ruddington; an amazing variety of these vehicles appeared, many having been damaged in road accidents. Returning south, this trip picked up the Tring and Bletchington gypsum. There was little plasterboard traffic and it might go on either trip according to its destination. The locos working these trips would normally be: Annesley - a 'K3', 'J39' or even a 'Scot'; Leicester - usually a 'B1', but they might commandeer a 'B16' off a York job.

The approach-lit signals at Hotchley Hill were a feature worthy of mention; most of the electric signals in the area were of this type. They were not like the approach-controlled junction signals now so common, but had no light at all until a train appeared. I was told that this came about as a result of Hotchley Hill box being burned down, and the current thinking was to introduce this method when the new box was built.

Passing through on freights the '9F' 2-10-0s predominated, of course. These fine locos worked most of the 'Windcutters', but '8Fs' began to appear and you could also see the occasional 'WD' or 'K3' on these trains. For a time there were some 'O1s' around on the Leicester turns but these, unfortunately, disappeared later.

There were three fitted freights from Dringhouses which came through about mid-morning going to Bristol, Cardiff and Banbury. The locos were a permutation of 'B1', 'B16' or 'V2', and I always looked forward to seeing them storming up the ruling gradient of 1 in 176. Needless to say, the '9Fs' were an equally stirring sight, but so common that you didn't notice them as much. In the early evening came the two fish trains - the 3.30 pm Hull to Plymouth and the 4.30 pm Grimsby to Whitland. Both were quite long trains which left behind a distinct aroma as they rushed along, and both hauled invariably by 'K3s'.

Butler Henderson was dragged through one bleak November afternoon on its way to Clapham Museum. Thankfully it is now able to work again. The same cannot be said, though, of the new 'Hymeks' which came past, light engine, each week on delivery to the Western Region, or most of the 30 classes of steam locos which I observed at East Leake. There were about 130 trains passing each day and practically all were steam.

To return now to the consignment notes. These were sent up to East Leake to be dealt with by the clerk. The average rate charged was about £1 per ton, which was quite a lot in those days. As we dispatched about 200 tons per day there was good revenue for such a small place. Invoices had to be sent to the destinations and the consignment notes then went to the Accounts Office. The gypsum was on a sort of pipeline basis - slow transits in old wagons - but there was sufficient arriving at the other end each day to keep them going, and it was a very basic raw material, no doubt being stockpiled for future use.

The passenger work involved a great deal of paperwork with the dreaded Monthly Returns having to be sent to Watford. The Station Master and clerk dealt with any other paperwork which included pay. An unusual feature on the London Midland Region, in which the GC line was by that time, was that salaried staff were paid fortnightly. I received the princely sum of about £28 for two weeks' work, but it was quite adequate for a single man living in digs. I even had money to spare! All the pay was worked out manually, including Income Tax, but it was no great task with only a handful of staff to be looked after.

We dealt with quite a lot of parcels traffic. A van came out from Nottingham on alternate days to deliver to local villages - Thrumpton, Barton-in-Fabis, Wymeswold. The squire of Thrumpton once gave me a half-crown tip (2s 6d, or 12.5p) when I carried his bag. This was on a Saturday afternoon when, as usual, I was covering the platform duties and booking tickets.

At East Leake goods yard the main traffic was perlite. This rather exotic item was apparently volcanic dust from Sardinia and arrived in shiploads at Boston Dock, where a train of 16-tonners was loaded and sheeted. Often the train would go through East Leake and run to Leicester so that it could return on the down road ready for propelling into the goods yard. This movement meant the porter or myself doing a bit of shunting. Delivery of the perlite was then by hired lorries to the Gotham works of British Plaster Board where it was mixed with the locally mined gypsum to make building plaster. The same works also made Plaster of Paris. I remember that the workers, including the landlord of my digs, used to go home covered in white dust every day.

On the down side was a recess siding, which was mainly used for stabling surplus mineral wagons. It was not often used for temporary recessing, ie to let another train pass, and there were two reasons for this. First, as it was on a down grade at this point, even long freight trains were running pretty quickly with, incidentally, a fairly high rate of hot axle boxes as a result. The Annesley men were in a hurry to get home! A hot box would result in recessing if the guard could attract the signalman's attention in time for him to 'throw the boards on' in front of the driver, or if the signalman was on his toes anyway. Second, to recess a long train meant drawing a long way down with the driver hanging out of the cab looking for the guard's hand signal. Then there was a long setting back movement with a good chance of demolishing the buffer stops.

Behind this siding was East Leake signal box, a pleasing structure of GC design. One of the signalmen came from Wiltshire, my present home, but I have little recollection of the other two who worked round the shifts to cover 24 hours. One of the relief signalmen was very popular as his son-in-law was the Notts Forest goalkeeper. Such is fame!

On the up side was another recess siding, kept clear for its proper purpose and frequently used by heavy coal trains which then restarted with a tremendous roar from the '9F' as there was still some way to go before reaching the summit at Barnston.

Gotham Sidings was a remote location and not part of my area except when I was 'on call'. I had a walk down there one lovely summer evening in 1962, the only access being by a long farm track from Gotham village. On arrival at the main line I found it to be an idyllic spot with buttercups, trees and fields as far as the eye could see, and lots of trains passing by. Apart from the last few passenger trains of the day there were several freights. At 6.20 pm, York 'B16' 4-6-0 No 61455 came through with the 4.50 pm Woodford Halse-Dringhouses Class C. A little later, of course, came the fish trains - No 61893 of Dairycoates was on the Hull and No 61939 of Immingham on the Grimsby.

One of the signalmen, who was 70 and lived in Gotham, had worked at the box since 1922. This span of 40 years, starting in Great Central days, also took in the whole of the LNER era and must have become monotonous, working the three shifts year in and year out. However, his evening was enlivened on one occasion when a tramp appeared. When asked who he was the man said he was a guard, but when the signalman asked where were his 'traps' (a guard's bag including flags, detonators and handlamp), he had to admit he was not a guard but was given a cup of tea and sent on his way. It was always the rule, of course, that no unau-

thorised person was allowed in the box.

All too soon it was time for me to go back, never to return. Ambition was calling and in March 1963 I moved on, although I had been asked to stay at East Leake. I sometimes wondered if I did the right thing, as the move to Elland brought a dramatic change and not always for the better.

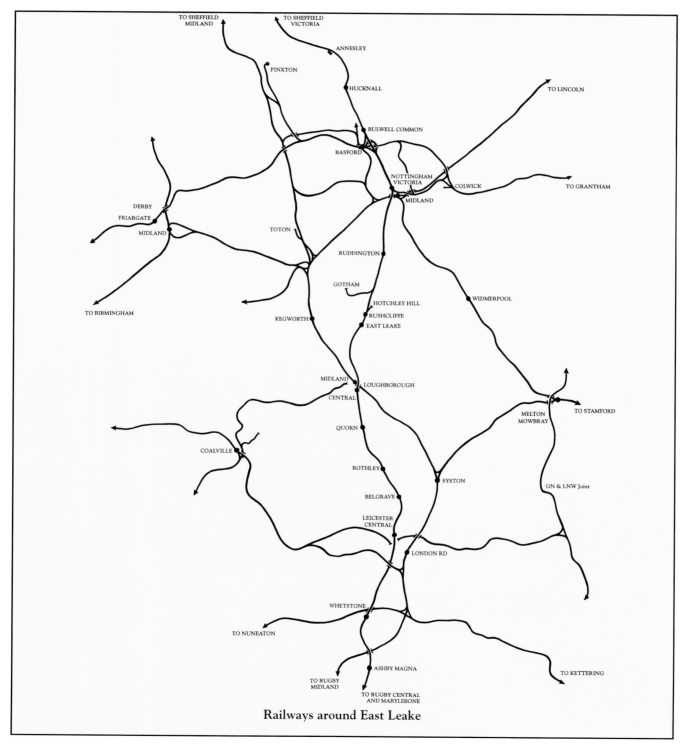

Railways around East Leake

'5MT' 4-6-0 No 73010, East Leake, 5.59 pm, 29.6.62, Darnall-Ruislip special

People travelling on 30-year-old Underground trains find it hard to believe that they were once the latest thing. They had aluminium bodies with no need to be painted, although such luxuries as air conditioning or good suspension were unheard of and they are now very long in the tooth. Several new sets as well as the new 'Hymeks' came through on the GC. Next to the loco is a brake van and an adaptor wagon for coupling to the Underground set. Such adaptors have to be used for a wide variety of coaches and wagons, for example EMU sets, tippler wagons with rotary couplers, etc, when going to the Works or in an emergency. The loco wears a 14D shedplate but '2F' has been chalked next to it.

No 73010 was the first Standard I ever saw, back in the early 1950s. I will never forget the excitement, looking through the window at the end of Platform 6 at Leeds City and seeing this loco with a large number plate on the smokebox.

'4F' 0-6-0 No 44539, Coalville LNW, 3.2 pm, 9.5.62

On the LNW line from Loughborough to Nuneaton, this is not a well-known location, although many people will be familiar with the other closed station at Coalville, scene of so many successful Open Days. Hopefully that station will reopen in the not too distant future. My visit to the station in the photo was purely on the off chance of finding something - I was often lucky in this way. Occasionally I had a Working Timetable for the relevant area and this helped. You could not guarantee, however, that a particular freight train would run on the day.

The station buildings and platform were still in good condition despite having been closed in 1941. Note the ground frame, with levers to control the points in the immediate vicinity, half hidden by the undergrowth, and the 'Wessy' signals in the distance.

'L1' 2-6-4T No 67785, West Hallam (for Dale Abbey), 4.30 pm, 23.5.62, 3.0 pm Grantham-Derby Friargate

This fairly industrial scene was, even then, declining. The colliery screens (loading point) are in the background, but like so many pits, even in the richly seamed Midlands, this one closed long ago. The Station Master, Mr Cave, is on duty on the platform; he was later to take over from me at East Leake. The driver is looking at those mysterious goings on under the engine which seemed to occupy so much time in steam days. Both platforms are tidy but the garden and tubs have yet to spring into life. Note the electric lamps on the loco - yet it always seemed odd that an oil lamp still had to be found to show the class of train! A white marker would have done just as well, but perhaps this was not worthwhile as so few locos had electric lamps fitted. I do not know what the old coach in the background, behind the platform, was doing. It looks like a Pooley's coach; these travelled around the country and visited any location where a weighbridge needed to be tested for accuracy. Inside the coach were test weights to compare with the performance of the equipment in the weighbridge. It must have been a nice job travelling around and doing this sort of work.

'B16' 4-6-0 No 61455, Gotham Sidings, 6.28 pm, 13.6.62, 4.50 pm Woodford-Dringhouses Class C
On a pleasant June evening I walked along the cart track to Gotham Sidings. The nearest road was a mile away, but one of the signalmen had walked or cycled there, rain or shine, for 40 years. 'B16s' were quite common on the GC main line - they were York engines that worked up each morning on fitted freights and returned later in the day, unless they were 'borrowed' in the meantime for a local job. A typical fitted freight consisting mainly of vans of sundries plus the odd container.

'Britannia' 4-6-2 No 70048 *The Territorial Army 1908-1958*, East Leake, 8.56 am, 30.6.62, 8.45 am Nottingham Victoria-Marylebone

'Britannias' seemed a strange choice to run the fairly pedestrian and lightly loaded Nottinghams; 'Black Fives' were better suited for these jobs, but the 'Britannias' introduced a bit of interest. At about this time 'Scots' also started to appear, displaced from elsewhere. No 70048 had one of the largest nameplates in the country at the time.

This view shows the up yard, used for the perlite wagons. A train of these had just arrived and the sheets are still in position. The shunting neck can be seen straight ahead; this is where 'B1' 4-6-0 No 61077 failed to hold a raft of perlite wagons and was pushed through the stops. These wagons had no automatic brake, that is one controlled by the driver. Only the handbrakes could be used and it was a slow business pinning these down.

'L1' 2-6-4T No 67767, East Leake, 5.53 pm, 23.7.62, 5.30 pm Nottingham Victoria-Rugby Central
This was the busy rush-hour train used by the East Leake commuters, and is here comprised of six coaches of mainly non-corridor stock. 'L1s' worked the two Nottingham-Rugby trains until the end of 1962, when they were withdrawn for scrap and replaced by Ivatt 2-6-0s, so they did not have a long life, only having been introduced in the late 1940s. In 1962 they were used extensively in the Nottingham area, particularly on the GN Grantham to Derby services. The GC locals were known as 'ORDs', being a diminutive of 'ordinary', to distinguish them from the express trains. Other locos used between Nottingham and Leicester were 'B1s' and 'Black Fives', and these had, of course, to be turned at each end of the short journey.

'B16' 4-6-0 No 61454, East Leake, 6.57 pm, 23.7.62, 4.50 pm Woodford-Dringhouses
The pallet vans which make up most of the train were withdrawn soon afterwards as they were found to be unstable at speed. In an earlier incident some of these 'palvans' were derailed approaching Barnston tunnel, in the distance; fortunately they derailed into the 'six foot' (between the tracks) so they missed the tunnel wall. They then crossed over to the 'cess' (nearside), and so avoided the island platform at East Leake. There was no escape, though, from the points beyond the station, where they ran amok. No 61454 is passing the change-of-gradient marker - having climbed to Barnston it is now downhill to Nottingham.

'B16' 4-6-0 No 61421, East Leake, 6.22 pm, 19.7.62, 4.50 pm Woodford-Dringhouses
A pleasant summer's evening at the south end of the station, where the lines widened out to accommodate the island platform. It was certainly worthwhile staying on after work when these sorts of train were around and in such an attractive setting. The main point of interest is the road tanker on the flat wagon - I do not know the story behind this, and it was not a very common sight, but it illustrates that heavy lorries have been carried by rail for many years.

'L1' 2-6-4T No 67786, Pye Hill and Somercotes, 6.28 pm, 13.7.62, 5.19 pm Bingham-Pinxton
This area of countryside was made famous by D. H. Lawrence. The Pinxton branch was rather an anachronism even in 1962. Whilst it ran through an industrial area, the stations were quite a long way from the towns they purported to serve; had its passenger service survived it would have had diesel units, obviating run-round problems with associated points and signals. A more frequent interval service would have been introduced and the stations reduced to unmanned platforms with shelters and maybe 'Park and Ride' car parks. The signal box appears to be switched out, but lines like this did tend to have rather a lot of expensive manned boxes. The double signals in the distance mark the busy Midland Erewash Valley line.

'6P/5F' 2-6-0 No 42971, Polesworth, 1.49 pm, 1.8.62, Down Class 6
One of the fascinating things about railway photography is that sometimes you can record changes just before or just after they happen. In this case the wires are up but the electric locos have not yet taken over.

These attractive Stanier locos were sometimes known as 'Stanier Crabs', I suppose because they followed the Hughes 2-6-0 'Crabs' numerically and had the same wheel arrangement. They did not, though, have the raised running board which gave rise to the latter's name. The train looks rather out of place now, consisting of vacuum-braked wagons; it was normal then but looks wrong in conjunction with the electrification.

'8F' 2-8-0 No 48640 and Bo-Bo No D5000, Hathern, 3.21 pm, 31.7.62
When I worked at East Leake it was pleasant to be able to go over, on my half day, to the nearby Midland main line, where there was always plenty of activity. This is one part of the Midland main line which has continued to be heavily used by freight, particularly MGR trains. D5000 was quite new at the time but the reason for it being hauled by the '8F' is a mystery.

'4MT' 2-6-0 No 43154, East Leake, 11.5 am, 28.2.63, 9.55 am Rugby Central-Nottingham Victoria
For well over 100 years local coal merchants could be seen carrying out their business in small station goods yards. They often rented a fixed space to stack their coal, as seen in the foreground here. There was a lot of heavy shovelling to be done in unloading the wagons, putting excess coal to stock, picking it up again and filling the bags. People of an older generation will remember counting the bags as they were delivered to their house.

The morning train from Rugby is at the platform in charge of an Ivatt 'Mogul' now that the 'L1s' have gone. The village road from East to West Leake goes under the line at this point and the porter's room, with its welcome roaring fire, hides the front of the loco. Behind me is the Station Master's house and wartime control office, later used for storing vermiculite. There is a housing estate on this site now.

'O1' 2-8-0 No 63676, East Leake, 1.20 pm, 31.3.62, Down Class K
East Leake station was set in pleasant surroundings. The village road to West Leake went under the north end of the platform and the south end benefited from the long gardens of the houses. The 'O1' is working a train which always conveyed a great mixture of traffic, but there is no vacuum brake pipe on the front of the loco despite its fairly modern appearance, being a Thompson rebuild of 1944 vintage. Your attention is directed to the sign which reads 'You may telephone from here'. The Station Master had to use this phone too!

'Black Five' 4-6-0 No 45223, Quorn and Woodhouse, 6.30 pm, 15.8.62, 5.5 pm Woodford Halse-Nottingham Victoria
Quorn is now better known than ever, but in 1962 it was a quiet sort of place and the station struggled to hang on to its infrequent local service. The 'ORD' has its normal type of motive power but the train is an odd mixture of BR and LNER coaches. On the platform are the usual GC 'London Extension' buildings, liberally supplied with posters. This was in the days when BR used its advertisement hoardings for pictures of BR ships and holiday towns served by rail. As it is summer there are quite a few empty coal trucks stabled in the yard in the left background.

'Hall' 4-6-0 No 7905 *Fowey Hall*, Banbury, 2.25 pm, 10.10.62, 10.8 am York-Bournemouth
The Bournemouth travelled up the GC main line then across to Banbury where the GW took over, so a change of loco was necessary. Going north, however, a 'Hall' would work as far as Leicester Central, while in some cases SR locos ran from Bournemouth to Oxford. The driver seems unconcerned that there is only one lamp instead of two on the buffer-beam, but there are a few minutes before departure time. Banbury's then very modern buildings contrast with the motive power, but the 'Hall' maintains the GW tradition of sparkling paintwork. A further quirk, although not evident in the photo, was the presence of GW signals in abundance, which were still there until the end of the days of the Class '50s'. There are cattle wagons on the right, demonstrating the rural nature of the area.

'28xx' 2-8-0 No 2834, Down Class 7, and '61xx' 2-6-2T No 6156, 4.4 pm Princes Risborough-Oxford, Oxford, 5.3 pm, 10.10.62
The low sun indicates that it is late afternoon. The main object of the photo was the Princes Risborough train at the platform but it was not in a very good spot. The passing long oil train does not have barrier wagons so, hopefully, is not conveying flammable goods. University term-time is just starting which accounts for the huge amounts of luggage on the platform; every type of barrow imaginable was pressed into use. Outside the station the number of bikes was beyond belief, many ridden at high speed by characters in gowns. Oxford station has, thankfully, been rebuilt twice since this photo was taken; in 1962 the waiting rooms were rather grotty and the first rebuilding was only of a temporary nature. Note the horse boxes on the left.

'8F' 2-8-0 No 48156, Widmerpool, 1.34 pm, 15.8.62, Down Class 7
A summer shower has just cleared, revealing a country station with virtually everything you would expect to see, even though it had been closed for some time. In the goods yard there is a weigh office, loading dock and traditional shed, the Midland signal box is manned, and the station buildings and fences are still intact. There are even several goods wagons around, but whether they were just stabled, like the coaching stock, or in use in unclear. From the position of the box vans it would seem that they, at least, were in traffic. Part of this line, then on the St Pancras-Nottingham route, is still used by the Research people; this was amply demonstrated by the test at Old Dalby when diesel No 46009 hit a nuclear flask at 100 mph. Such concerns, however, were a long way off in 1962 as No 48156 trundles along with a tender full of coal and a long rake of empty mineral wagons.

'4MT' 2-6-4T No 42618, Linby, 3.44 pm, 13.2.63, 3.11 pm Nottingham Midland-Worksop
It is a bitterly cold afternoon during a winter long remembered for its severity. Most of the snow has been cleared from the platforms, which at Linby were staggered, resulting in the station buildings being at ground level away from the platforms. There is a gateway leading to a cattle dock and weighbridge, and in the background are some colliery sidings.

'B1' 4-6-0 No 61024 *Addax*, Gotham, 12.34 pm, 8.3.63, 9.42 am from Queens Walk
This was the very last train at Gotham. When passenger stations closed the event was usually well publicised and resulted in hundreds of people milling about, but so far as I know I was the only witness of this closure. The 'B1' eventually collected several more wagons which had been standing about for some time and then departed from the village of the Cuckoo Bush, where cheeses were, at one time, rolled down a hill once a year chased by the local populace.

'Jubilee' 4-6-0 No 45624 *St Helena*, Gotham, 11.59 am, 20.2.63, 9.42 am Queens Walk-Gotham
Rather a bleak outlook on a winter's day is enlivened by the unique visit of a 'Jubilee' to the Gotham branch. *St Helena*, blocking the country road from East Leake, is propelling 'shocvans' (vans fitted with shock-absorbing equipment) into the Plaster Board's siding, where they are needed to carry traffic indicated by the firm's name. I normally saw this operation on the way to my lodgings for lunch, and it wasn't unusual for the road traffic to be stopped. 'L1s' or Ivatt 2-6-0s were more normal motive power for the daily trip.

'O1' 2-8-0 No 63777, Kimberley, 2.14 pm, 14.2.62, Class J westbound

How not to do it (2)! The low winter sun meant that the shadow from the telegraph pole was not obvious until a train came along, and then it was too late if the train was interesting enough for a photo. To make life a little easier for the crew of the 'O1' when running tender first, they have a sheet stretching from cab to tender. Note the odd-looking barrow in the distance and a gate at the bottom of the footbridge steps. This fine-sounding station and its line have now gone.

'O1' 2-8-0 No 63578, Hucknall Town, 2.50 pm, 14.2.62, Down Class H

The Annesley-Woodford 'Windcutters' are well known, but not all started or terminated at Annesley; some finished their journeys at collieries in the area north of Nottingham or at Hucknall Town. This 'O1' is moving empties to a local colliery, and as usual for the locality 16-ton mineral wagons predominate, and there are more in the sidings to the left. This line was one of three at Hucknall running parallel, and although the station buildings still existed there was no longer a passenger service.

'4MT' 2-6-4T No 42618, Hucknall Byron, 3.41 pm, 14.2.62, 3.11 pm Nottingham Midland-Worksop

The Midland was not given to building many single-island platform stations such as this, but it would not be confused with the nearby GC station due to the style of architecture - note the rather fine chimneys. It was appropriate that this station acquired such a distinctive name, after the local poet.

The signal box sits at the end of the platform and collieries are much in evidence from the slag heaps and rows of empty wagons to be seen. The fence beside the train marks the dividing line between BR and NCB property. It is mid-afternoon but the two official-looking men are awaiting the train - perhaps they are BR auditors returning home? Note that main-line stock is in use on this local train.

'Britannia' 4-6-2 No 70028 *Royal Star*, Kegworth, 2.30 pm, 11.4.62, 12.10 pm Manchester Piccadilly-St Pancras
As well as making a fine show, *Royal Star* is working a train via a rather unusual route. According to my notes it travelled from Manchester Piccadilly calling at Stoke and Derby on its way to St Pancras. Midland signals were still in use and a platelayer's trolley lies in the '10 foot' (the middle area in a four-track line) - its wheels have been removed and left there, and is the sort of item that vandals would nowadays make use of. Today Ratcliffe MGR Power Station dominates this area. Red Hill tunnels, approaching the Trent river bridge, are in the background.

Lady Angela, **Kingston on Soar, 1.17 pm, 10.12.62**
Gypsum was the main traffic in the Kegworth as well as the East Leake areas. At Kegworth a private loco took over the empty wagons from BR and went off through the woods to a mine near Kingston on Soar. This pleasant kind of scene was fairly common in the Midlands, with many private steam locos being used for ironstone or gypsum workings. The type of road crossing, though, was not up to BR standards.

'L1' 2-6-4T No 67741, Basford North, 6.4 pm, 23.7.60, 5.19 pm Bingham-Pinxton
Basford North was a busy junction. The lines going away to the left joined the GC main line at Bulwell, while behind the train was a very interesting three-tier crossing - the line on the left of the 'L1' dived under the GC main line before joining it over to the right at Bagthorpe Junction. There was a further junction behind the train taking two more lines under the GC at the middle level and continuing to Colwick. The Pinxton branch disappeared long ago and so, later, did the other lines in the area including, of course, the GC.

Note the point mechanism in the left foreground: the facing point lock between the rails; detection for the signalling beside the track, actuated by interlocking between the point rod and signal wire; and a fouling bar in rear of the turnout against the left-hand rail - the points could not be moved if train wheels were depressing this bar. In most places today all this is done electronically. Other items of interest are the lamps and signals in the distance. Altogether this is a view which holds the attention, even though it was merely intended at the time as a record shot of the Pinxton train.

'J6' 0-6-0 No 64273, Derby Friargate, 10.47 am, 21.4.56, 9.30 am Nottingham Victoria-Derby Friargate

Although I lived within sound, if not quite within sight, of the NER Leeds-Harrogate line, it was the GN which captured my imagination, and this is one of my favourite photos of a GN loco; somebody has taken the trouble to clean the early BR totem on the tender. Perhaps the 'J6s' were not designed for local passenger working, but they did steady work on this type of job in the East Midlands for many years, although there is the obvious problem of having to turn the loco frequently. Here the uncoupling operation, as ever, attracts its share of onlookers.

Note the legend 'Basford North Link A', the screw coupling and vacuum and heating pipes on the block-ended coach alongside. The metal plate showed the coach's measurements and net weight, which was useful if you wished to time the train and record the load pulled by the loco.

'3MT' 2-6-2T No 40050, Nottingham Midland, 7.8 pm, 23.7.60, 7.5 pm (SO) to Worksop

Fowler Class '3' tanks were not very common and this one is being recorded by short-trousered trainspotters while on the other side the shunter advises the driver that the train is coupled up ready for departure - a little late. Overhead is the GC main line, now gone. An early DMU occupies the middle road and, on the left, is a train from Worksop on which I had been lucky enough to have a footplate trip from Radford; the fireman had observed me taking a photo of his train at Bulwell Market and, as he was keen on photography, invited me up for the short trip to Nottingham.

'J6' 0-6-0 No 64235, empty stock, and 'V2' 2-6-2 No 60877, Up 'South Yorkshireman', Nottingham Victoria, 12.39 pm, 24.7.57

I once made a point of travelling the full distance from Bradford Exchange to Marylebone on the 'South Yorkshireman'; it was a long, rather slow journey by today's standards but very interesting. The GN 'J6' loco is a reminder that this joint station saw a great deal of GN as well as GC activity. On this particular day it was very busy as there was a bus strike in progress and long trains hauled by 'J6s' or the odd ex-GC 'Director' brought in hundreds of passengers. Note the two sets of coaches in 'plum and spilt milk' livery (I must say that I prefer this more flowery description to another sometimes used). A few minutes later I was taking another photo from the platform on the left when I was informed, by a railway policeman, that photography was not allowed, so I left! Sad to think that Victoria station has now disappeared completely.

'J39' 0-6-0 No 64818, Rushcliffe Halt, 2.20 pm, 3.7.62, 1.7 pm Queens Walk-Hotchley Hill
The 'J39' is propelling a string of empty hopper and 16-ton mineral wagons into the sidings of British Plaster Board at Hotchley Hill where they will each be swept out by one of the firm's employees to remove any scrap metal or coal dust before loading with gypsum for cement making. In the background is Hotchley Hill signal box which was opened for a couple of hours each afternoon for this trip, which also took out the northbound traffic - mainly for Hope and Penyffordd. A little later a 'B1' would appear with the Ruddington-Leicester trip to take out the southbound gypsum - mainly for Tring and Bletchington; the small hopper wagons next to the loco were used for the latter and worked in circuit, but the 16-tonners were mainly from coal workings and were collected from Gotham Sidings by the trip seen here. Note the approach-lit signal seen above the footbridge - it showed no light until a train approached, which was rather unusual and not to be found nowadays. The station platforms have lamp cases for the only means of lighting - paraffin lamps. It is not the normal type of GC island platform as it was built later to serve the local golf course.

'5MT' 4-6-0 No 73066, Quorn, 5.46 pm, 15.8.64, 12.27 pm Margate-Nottingham Victoria additional
Quorn looks very neglected after closure, and some years before it will become part of the revived Great Central Railway. It is always sad to see a station in this state especially when the line is still in use as it was in 1964. The booking office, timetable board and roof are still intact, but there are weeds growing on the platform. As it is a Summer Saturday there are plenty of trains about including this special, indicated by the '1X20' board on the smokebox. The Standard Class '5s' were fine-looking locos and were more successful and long lived than many of the Standard types.

'Britannia' 4-6-2 No 70048 *The Territorial Army 1908-1958*, **Belgrave and Birstall, 5.49 pm, 15.8.62, 5.20 pm Nottingham Victoria-Marylebone**
This is a locality which has now returned to life with the opening of the preserved Great Central Railway's new Leicester North station and the service to Loughborough. It was a photogenic spot in 1962 with a convenient footpath alongside the line. The station entrance was on the bridge with steps down to the standard GC island platform.
    The platform edge has been whitened to a high standard. At Rushcliffe the porter often complained about the quality of the brushes for this job: 'They don't make them like they used to,' he would say. As he actually worked for the original GC, perhaps he was entitled to say so!

'K3' 2-6-0 No 61857, East Leake, 4.49 pm, 7.7.62, 11.0 am (SO) Bournemouth Central-Sheffield Victoria
Hauling a typical Summer Saturday GC train, No 61857 carries a 50B (Hull) shedplate; the first coach is of LMS vintage. The train is running downhill at the ruling gradient of 1 in 176 and the loco is starting to blow off steam.

Note the two-wheel barrow and lamp case with built-in station name. The hanging baskets were, unfortunately, not a great success in the station gardens contest - perhaps this was because we put them up just after the judges had made their surprise visit! In any event they did not compare very well with the lavish displays put on at some stations (show-offs!), but at least it showed willing as the station had not often been entered before. The Station Master himself ended up having to foot the bill for the baskets.

8

Elland i/c Greetland

March 1963 to April 1964

Early in 1963 I had a interview at Wakefield for the job of Station Master/Goods Agent at Elland, also in charge of Greetland. It was a return home, as the Trains Office job 14 months earlier had been in the same District, but the Divisional organisation was to take over in 1964, getting rid of the three Districts - Leeds, Wakefield and York.

It might be of interest to readers to have a look at how Station Masters were selected. The one definite requirement was that you had passed an Oral Block examination with a District Inspector - this consisted of going through your knowledge of the Rule Book, Block Regulations, General Appendix, etc. No matter how well you might have done in a written exam at evening classes, the oral exam was a must. Drivers, guards, signalmen and many others have to go through a similar process, concentrating, of course, on the areas affecting their jobs. Later I was to take the Knottingley guards in their bi-annual exams, which included showing them track circuit clips, which were then new - one clip was clamped on to each rail, and they were connected by a wire between them. This put the signal in rear to danger to protect a mishap. They were quite easy to put on but very difficult to get off again.

Also, at SM interviews you were expected to show some knowledge of commercial work. At one time this was not considered so important, and many signalmen were able to become SMs due to their operating knowledge, and would pick up the booking office and goods office work later.

Finally at the interview, there were the traditional questions about an SM's visits to signal boxes. Those adjacent to the station had to be visited daily, and any which were further afield once a week, apart from the pay visit on Thursday. You had to go through a sort of checklist at the interview: look at the train register and make sure it reflects the current situation and matches with the positions of the block instruments when you walk into the box; check the

flags, the detonators (ensuring they are not beyond the time span allowed since manufacture), and the handlamp (which should be lit if after dark), make sure the stores and equipment are adequate, everything is clean and tidy, the seals are not broken on signal release boxes, etc.

You then had to listen to the grumbles. Like the British soldier of ancient tradition, most signalmen and, even more so, crossing keepers had their grouses although, to be fair, there were some who were always cheerful, while the others sometimes had good reason to complain. For the most part it was at quiet locations, where people spent a lot of time alone and with little to do but think, that most problems occurred.

At the interviews one District Operating Superintendent even expected you to say that the first thing to do was to see that the signalman was present and in a fit state to carry out his duties, not asleep, etc.

Elland was on the busy former Lancashire & Yorkshire Railway main line, but the two stations, Elland and Greetland, had closed. My office was on the island platform at Elland, but it was a very different situation from the GC island platform at East Leake. At the tail end of that bitter winter of 1963 it was grim indeed, literally amongst the 'dark satanic mills'. Elland signal box was quite new, having replaced the two older boxes. The odd thing was that semaphore signals had been retained on the up side (up to Manchester, of course) but electric ones were installed on the down.

One of the main purposes of the job was to look after the Power Station traffic and its attendant paperwork. This involved two clerks dealing with mountains of labels, one from each wagon of the four or five trains a day, and checking them against the invoices. As the two young lads spent a lot of time fooling around, I decided that I could manage with just one - the better one! Although this meant the saving of a job and the cost involved, I did not endear myself to the Divisional staff people by suggesting that the other clerk be sent to a passenger station to widen his knowledge, and that I wouldn't want him back!

I had to do quite a lot of shunting, particularly to cover a vacancy when the shunter left BR. Most of it was at Greetland where there was a large ground-frame situated in a hut - indeed, almost a mini signal box. This controlled the Engineers sidings, used to stable wagons ready for weekend work but also involving movements in and out during the week.

It was decided that the station buildings at Elland should be demolished and we (the remaining clerk, a checker and a shunter) should move to the old goods office which was situated, traditionally, on the end of the warehouse. The warehouse was leased to a private firm and the goods office had not been used for many years. It was winter, and although a small gas fire was installed it heated only a small proportion of the office. The old sloping desks were refurbished by covering the tops with lino! Behind the skirting boards the large mouse population scuttled about.

There were several jobs to be done on a regular basis which were fairly typical of an SM's duties in those days.

Pay

The local staff, including the platelayers, collected theirs from the office, but I had to take the pay for the Greetland staff by taxi each Thursday morning. This was a standing arrangement and, in the days when few people used taxis, I normally travelled in a wedding/funeral car which created quite an impression when I arrived at Greetland No 2 signal box. Going back I had, of course, to walk. Usually I went through the tunnel, of 420 yards. I do not know whether this was allowed in the Rules but, if pushed, I could claim to be checking on the state of the safety recesses inside the tunnel, the sentry-box-size holes in the tunnel walls. I certainly had to make regular use of them when one, or often two, steam trains came through, filling the tunnel with smoke for several minutes.

Collecting outstanding accounts

Many freight customers were slow to pay their bills and I received a long list every month from the Centralised Accounts Office at Huddersfield. This was a bit of a problem as there was a large area to cover with no transport available. In any case, I had no idea what the bills were about - they were just names and amounts. For the most part they were for Sundries dealt with by Halifax, which covered the Elland area for collections and deliveries. Usually the firms were cooperative, as it saved them having to post a cheque. I trudged round to their offices and could give them a receipt for the money. More diffi-

cult was collecting passenger fares where people had been allowed to travel on the promise of payment later. Invariably they did not want to pay later! All sorts of excuses were made. 'The train was late so why should I have to pay for it?' 'I did not have any money then and I do not have any now either!' 'I am not paying because the fares are too high!'

Claims inspections

I often had this job as an SM or clerk. Generally it was an easy task to go to a factory or house to examine some goods damaged in transit. Elland, however, was the home of one of the largest manufacturers of fire extinguishers in the country. Visits there were frequent and could be difficult as it was necessary for me to ask to check their books to see that claims for items lost in transit were at the true cost of the goods. In any case there was always a lot of paperwork involved.

To enliven the scene there was a wide variety of loco types. 'WDs' predominated on freights, with 'B16s', '8Fs', '4Fs' and 'Crabs' also appearing in quite large numbers. Fowler and Stanier Class '4' tanks worked the passenger and parcels trains, while 'Jubilees' came through on Summer Saturday seaside trains; I worked every Saturday morning and looked forward to seeing these locos. The odd 'Scot' appeared, mainly on freight, and this continued the practice I had seen at East Leake. Inspection Saloons sometimes called in, worked by a wide variety of locos, but at least you knew, from the circulars, when they were due. I once had the galling experience of being invited into the Saloon when it spent an hour at Elland. I was told that I could have some lunch with the guard, but as I had already eaten my usual sandwiches I had to decline and spent the hour chatting to the guard instead whilst the bigwigs had their lunch in grand style next door. It's strange to think that some of the old pre-war attitudes persisted into the 1950s and '60s. I suppose it was because most of the higher management was of the pre-war, pre-nationalisation breed and found it hard to accept the need for a more liberal regime. They were brought up in the days when jobs weren't openly advertised - you were asked to take promotion if thought suitable, or you might be sent to a station many miles away, whether you liked it or not.

It was an interesting job at Elland, with a number of new features which helped widen my experience, but I was not sorry when the job disappeared, and me with it, in May 1964. This was due to the opening of Healey Mills new yard which resulted in a reorganisation of local jobs. Area Management was some way off in the NE Region but already a merging of SM jobs was taking place. Mine was split up between Brighouse and Sowerby Bridge.

'B16' 4-6-0 No 61464, Elland, 9.11 am, 25.3.63, 7.0 am Mirfield-Mytholmroyd
The contrast between East Leake and Elland could hardly have been greater - I now found myself surrounded by smoky mills. Although Elland was another station with an island platform, this one was grim indeed. Partly this was due to the fact that it was now closed and the subway was full of rubbish instead of echoing to the sounds of passengers' footsteps.

Note the transformer wagon in the background and the anchor wagons full of stone, which were needed when transferring a transformer from road to rail (see also page 146). Next to the tender is a fog hut with its brazier, and a lever for the detonators. Later all the station buildings were demolished - if you visit the scene now all you will see will be two lines and the ever-encroaching undergrowth.

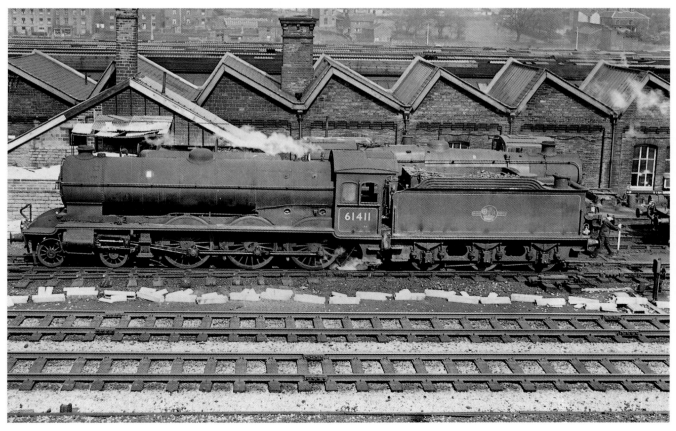

'J11' 0-6-0 No 64452, Penistone, 4.25 pm, 10.6.54

Here we see a metamorphosis from steam to electric which seemed to promise great things but, within 30 years, even the new electric locos had disappeared. The Penistone area was pure GC until 1954. I visited the station with friends just before the new electrics took over and we were disappointed to find that practically all the non-stop flow of freight trains consisted of two Robinsons on the front and one on the back. The air was black with smoke, but where were the new locos? Wouldn't we give our back teeth to go back there now and see either the steam or the electrics? The station has survived, although it was touch and go at one time.

'B16' 4-6-0 No 61411, Mirfield Shed, 2.8 pm, 15.4.61

The cascading of steam locos in the closing years was as interesting as, say, that of HSTs today - how else would you have several NER 'B16s' in traditional L&Y main-line territory? Mirfield had some to work mainly local freight trains. It presents quite a contrast to the Standard Class '5' and the '03' diesel shunter glimpsed behind it. I don't know why the shed roof was built to this shape, but there were some strange loco sheds around. The maintenance facilities were generally rather primitive. As a person with little knowledge of technical or footplate matters, I often wondered how they managed to keep going and provide such a good service.

Behind me was the remains of the Midland Railway line to Huddersfield, built, at great expense and involving heavy earthworks and bridges, purely in pursuance of the Midland's ambitions to have a share in traffic to the major towns in the area. It was not a success.

Blackpool Shed, 5.20 pm, 2.4.61

A visit to Blackpool, in the course of doing casual work on a buffet car on a train from Leeds, enabled me to see the incredible amount of activity at the resort. The new Class '31' diesel is a sign of things to come. Is it a coincidence that it is displaying a Class '9' indication? This is the sort of work that these locos now undertake, ie Engineers trains. It also has a tail lamp. Other classes pressed into passenger service were 'K3s' from Yorkshire and '8Fs' and 'Crabs' on East Lancashire excursions.

'Black Five' 4-6-0 No 44869 and 'Jubilee' 4-6-0 No 45552 *Silver Jubilee*, Farnley Junction, 7.25 pm, 15.8.60, 4.13 pm Newcastle-Liverpool Lime Street
This was the only chance I had of taking a photo of the first 'Jubilee'. The location was one well known to me - Farnley Junction shed, where many a Sunday was spent walking up and down the rows of locos inside. There was always a stale, smoky aroma, which was not unique to this shed. *Silver Jubilee* appears to be doing most of the work, almost pushing the 'Black Five', you might say, but appearances can be deceptive. The last unrebuilt 'Scot' (No 46156) was a regular performer on this job less than 10 years previously. The third line from the left is part of the flying junction of the 'New Line' from Huddersfield via Spen Valley.

'B16' 4-6-0 No 61464, Healey Mills, 3.43 pm, 28.10.61, 3.45 pm Class F to Stockton
This is Healey Mills before modernisation, which took place soon afterwards as part of the NE Region marshalling yard plan. Some people said these yards came too late, but when you remember that dieselisation was in full swing, there was some sense to it; there was no point in building large numbers of expensive diesels to work the innumerable inter-yard trips between places only a few miles apart. The West Riding and Carlisle were just two examples of where one big yard cut down on trip working, closed many small yards and introduced modern methods of working and, of course, modern staff facilities.

'B1' 4-6-0 Nos 61069 and 61024 *Addax*, Mirfield, 2.29 pm, 15.4.61, 2.15 pm (SO) Wakefield Kirkgate-Manchester Victoria
This train was always double-headed, as were many others on this stretch of line, which also carried the LNW Leeds-Liverpool services. The Mirfield 'speed signalling', as represented by the two signals behind the train, was very unusual. This system, although similar in some ways to that on the Euston-Watford DC local line, nevertheless had some unique features. Another singular point about this locality was the signalman poet - Walter Nugent Sinkinson of Heaton Lodge signal box. I have a copy of one of his books of poems, and very good they are too. Signalmen were often a contemplative lot, spending many hours quite alone, especially at night. The coaling stage in the background has a water tank on top and stands at the entrance to Mirfield shed yard.

'A3' 4-6-0 No 60083 *Sir Hugo*, Cardigan Road, 11.19 am, 8.9.60, 8.55 am Newcastle-Liverpool
Sir Hugo has nearly finished his part of the journey and it is easy going now to Leeds City. For many years these trains were double-headed by a 'D20' or 'D49' with a 'Pacific' or 'V2', as well as being tandem west of Leeds using LMS locos. The engine is in the double chimney condition but without the German-style smoke deflectors which some liked and some hated. Note the fine NER signals. The signal box was switched out most of the time, as was Armley, the next one towards Leeds, so the double signal was normally in this state. Coal was unloaded in the flat yard as well as on drops that stood behind me. A new station (Burley Park) has now been opened beyond the bridge and is a success even though only a 5-minute run from Leeds station.

'Jubilee' 4-6-0 No 45632 *Tonga*, Huddersfield, 9.7 am, 9.10.63, 8.2 am Stockport-Leeds parcels
Huddersfield had the almost archetypal large goods warehouse, and you can appreciate how intimidating such a place appeared to a young member of staff. Large numbers of people, both clerical and wages grades, were employed, and the man in charge - the Goods Agent - was very important indeed. This depot had the benefit of being next to the passenger station and near the town centre; usually such places were hidden away in an industrial area, a tram ride away from the shops. There are plenty of brake vans standing about. For many years an L&Y saddle tank could be seen shunting here.

'4F' 0-6-0 No 44098, Luddendenfoot, 3.25 pm, 15.10.61, 2.15 pm (Suns) Normanton-Manchester Victoria
This is a traditional West Riding scene. I visited the station on a rather dreary Sunday afternoon as the job of Station Master had been advertised and I was interested. Like many others, the job was withdrawn without being filled. However, as a Relief Station Master friend commented, 'It's the sort of place where the porter chops firewood on the SM's desk!', so maybe I was not missing much. The '4F' is making good progress on a little-used Sunday train; shortly afterwards DMUs took over most of the local services. There is a gas lamp and remains of a flower bed - it probably succumbed to the soot! It has been said that Bramwell Bronte worked at Luddendenfoot as a clerk.

'4MT' 2-6-4T No 42406, Elland, 3.42 pm, 3.4.63, 2.30 pm Normanton-Halifax parcels
The Fowler tank could not really have had a shorter train for this parcels job, but the line had lost its DMU local service so a separate train was provided. As mentioned before, the station was by now closed but still intact with myself and staff accommodated in the buildings on the island platform. In the background near the signal box a transformer is being transferred from road to rail and the two anchor wagons are fulfilling their purpose in the up loop. Note the old coach on the right with its clerestory roof - this and the other coach held equipment for the out-of-gauge movement of the transformer, destined for Elland Power Station, hidden behind the mill.

'3MT' 2-6-2T No 40117, Horbury and Ossett, 2.43 pm, 2.9.61, 2.22 pm Normanton-Sowerby Bridge
The most notable item in this photo is the permanent way ~ it is absolutely immaculate, with the shoulders of the ballast trimmed to form a perfect edge. And instead of stones or bits of sleepers, etc, there are flower tubs between the tracks; an effort has been made with the flower bed on the platform too. All this just a short distance from Healey Mills yard. The signalling and pointwork in the distance is very complex with the line to Barnsley going off to the right. Note the booking office window in the end of the station buildings, and 'Stands the clock at (nearly) ten to three', as in the Rupert Brooke poem.

'Crab' 2-6-0 No 42725, Crofton-Mytholmroyd freight, and 'B16' 4-6-0 No 61449, 7.0 am Mirfield-Mytholmroyd, Elland, 10.10 am, 19.4.63

This is rather a trick shot, and intentionally so! There are, of course, two trains, but the trigger was pressed at precisely the right moment to make it appear as a double-header. Both 'boards' are 'off' for the 'Crab', but the 'B16' languishes in the loop. It does, however, illustrate one of the features of the period. Both trains are going to Mytholmroyd - hardly the centre of the Universe, but a convenient marshalling yard to which traffic could be moved as part of the overall exercise of getting from A to B. The driver has spotted the photographer and is about to point him out to Guard Jim Harker, who is leaning casually against the tender. The water crane on the left was not used a great deal as the '4F' shunting pilot stood at Greetland for most of the day and only visited Elland for an hour or so to shunt the yard.

In the foreground are four empty wagons ready for loading with firebricks for dispatch to loco sheds around the country. All four are different; the one on the right is distinctive as it is a shock absorbing wagon, indicated by the three white lines. In those days a trip of, say, 100 miles might involve visits to half a dozen marshalling yards. Some could be hump yards and all would involve loose shunting of some sort, hence the need to try to avoid damage.

'4F' 0-6-0 No 43968, Greetland, 10.58 am, 20.7.63

It is a hot Summer Saturday and even the Calder Valley can look exotic on such a day! The '4F' is hurrying along with a short banana special for Halifax, the brake van, of course, completing the ensemblage - all freight trains needed one in those days. About five years later it was decided that fully-fitted trains, soon to be the norm, would not require them, and this made life a lot easier. Many were the cancellations and disgruntled customers due to lack of brake vans or late starts due to looking for them. Many were the Sundays spent, at great expense, in carrying out brake van censuses all over the country.

Bananas generally arrived at either Barry or Garston Docks. I don't know why these two in particular, but such traffic put in an appearance at certain times of the year until the 1970s. Now it goes by road.

9
Relief Station Master
May-September 1964

If you were made redundant as a Station Master, it was quite common to be offered a relief job covering holidays, vacancies, sickness, etc; many of these jobs were for the duration of the summer only. Strictly speaking I was not redundant, as both the East Leake and Elland posts were temporary due to their short-term nature; my substantive post was still in the Trains Office, despite my absence of 2½ years. I was very pleased to accept the job as Relief Station Master as it offered a variety of work and was good experience. I could also take my camera with me! The work did not only mean covering SM jobs but also clerical, as can be seen from the following list:

1.6.64-19.6.64

Wagon Distribution in the District Office at Wakefield Westgate This was rather difficult and boring work, consisting of taking phone calls from locations around the District which gave details of what vehicles they chose to declare as being on hand, spare, etc. There was no way of checking the details apart from routine visits by Wagon Inspectors who did spot checks, mainly at collieries - this was important as the NCB figures not only made up a large part of the total District position, but were also used for charging standage. It was a massive job, as even a place like Glasshoughton, now closed, took a whole day, there were so many wagons on hand. By about 4 pm we had built up a District figure to send by telex to London, but the whole thing was, by that time, many hours out of date and based on some pretty doubtful figures anyway.

20.6.64-4.7.64

Carcroft This was an insignificant station near Doncaster - today you can see the remains of the station from a Leeds-King's Cross train. At that time, however, there was a local passenger service, a few signal boxes and collieries. Thorpe Marsh Power Station, several miles away and which I didn't manage to visit, was served by '9Fs' hauling trains of 24½-ton hoppers. A small yard, at Castle Hills on the main line, served the branch to Brodsworth Colliery. This was one of the largest in the country and there were many shunting mishaps involving the large number of trains at Castle Hills. I had to deliver a Form 1 to a shunter during my brief stay - this was a disciplinary form and was an occupational hazard when a man worked at a place with a lot of potential for things to go wrong. Castle Hills was such a place. Thankfully the days of loose shunting of unfitted wagons are now over.

I had some miners' Guaranteed excursions one Saturday, then had to rush over to the Stainforth line where a cow had strayed on to the track. This involved trudging across several fields to the nearest farm to get someone to collect the cow. It turned out not to be his when I identified it as being of black and white appearance, but he took it to his neighbour's farm anyway which got me out of a spot. After this was another rush to cover the job at Castleford Cutsyke for the afternoon. Why this was necessary I don't know, as there was absolutely nothing happening. It did come in useful, however, as I was later to become SM at Castleford Central, covering quite a large area including the delightful Cutsyke district which had a coking plant at one end and a glass works at the other.

7.7.64-10.7.64

Wellington Street wagon clerk This was the only time I visited this large depot. My uncle worked at the adjacent Claims Office at the end of a 50-year spell on the railways, almost entirely at Hunslet Lane.

I spent some time there in 1967 and discovered an old notice advertising the office outing to Ireland in 1935. For a joke I pinned it up on the notice board and several people came along and said they had taken part in the trip over 30 years previously. Such was progress in the Goods Department, a world of its own employing vast numbers of people, yet largely unrecorded. My job for four days there was to collate the wagon situation and advise Wakefield, where my figures were disbelieved by the people I had been working with a few weeks previously!

14.7.64-24.7.64

Elland (but covering the clerical job described in the Elland chapter) At least I was able to see things from a different angle - it isn't often you get the chance to do a job which you had previously supervised.

27.7.64-29.7.64

Cleckheaton This was a rather unreal spell of three days on a line now disappeared, as has the adjacent 'New Line' - they both followed the Spen Valley and at one time had competing stations. The table below illustrates the extensive freight service in the area but, of course, the goods depots served had their own managers. Certainly the job I was covering was very quiet with the occasional signal box visit and pay arrangements to make. Similarly, a Saturday morning at Heckmondwike, on the same line, was hardly taxing.

4.8.64

Robin Hood This was an interesting day visiting my old haunts, including Lofthouse on the main Doncaster line. There is not much you can do in one day, though - it was just a case of being there to deal with any problems, which is what being an RSM often consisted of.

5.8.64-8.8.64

Crofton Junction Yard It was back to clerical work again here, mainly pay and rostering details. There was, however, a minor crisis as one day's pay for guards for the previous week was missing. The reason was that their pay was on the basis of daily returns being sent in to a centralised pay office. Unfortunately the previous Saturday's return had been lost and it nearly caused a riot! The yard was due to close so a lot of vacancies had not been filled and the remaining staff worked long hours and rest days. They expected to be paid promptly, and it put the Yard Master on the spot. He was walking a tightrope as it was, to keep the job ticking over. To alleviate the situation some emergency cash had to be hastily summoned.

The yard was a rarity - a gravity yard with no pilot. The method was for the wagons to be gravitated into the various sidings with consequent and frequent violent bangs as a raft of wagons collided with others already in the siding. There was no shortage of coal here for the office fires!

10.8.64-19.8.64

Horbury This was another goods office job but enlivened by being located on the island platform near the entrance to Healey Mills Yard and the Chas Roberts Wagon Works. Another RSM was covering the Station Master's job, and he upset the local staff by turning up to cover, on his own, a Sunday excursion. He did not claim any pay for this on the grounds that few passengers were expected and if he or the regular staff claimed Sunday pay the excursion's call at Horbury would make a loss.

20.8.64

Mirfield This was a day spent almost entirely on paying out the numerous staff employed in the area.

Freight services at Cleckheaton, 27.7.64

Time	Loco	Line	Train
9.11 am	61218	Down	P35 trip
9.23 am	45208	Down	8.10 am Healey Mills-Cleckheaton
10.02 am	44056	Down	9.25 am Healey Mills-Halifax
10.33 am	61338	Up	Light engine
11.13 am	90684	Down	Empty stock to Laisterdyke
11.22 am	61338	Down	8.50 am Normanton-Sowerby Bridge parcels
12.26 pm	90430	Down	11.20 pm Healey Mills-Laisterdyke
1.33 pm	90089	Down	1.20 pm Healey Mills-Cleckheaton
3.32 pm	90684	Down	2.45 pm Healey Mills-North Bridge

Each man identified himself by the antiquated system of producing his L&Y railway metal pay check, a circular piece of metal with his own pay number stamped on it. I can't imagine that this system lasted much longer, and I have certainly never since come across it.

21.8.64

Huddersfield I had a complete change here, illustrating the appeal of being an RSM. A passenger census was in operation. Nowadays, as you travel around, you have probably seen train conductors counting their passengers and perhaps using a clicker device to do this. Details are fed in to the TOPS computer system on a regular basis but, in 1964, you employed anyone available to stand on the platform at larger stations and count the people getting on and off trains. The aim was, of course, the same - to ensure that future services were planned to meet demand - and it was therefore a worthwhile exercise.

22.8.64

Horsforth To bring to an end a very varied and fascinating week came another brief Saturday morning session but particularly important to me as it also covered Headingley where my trainspotting days had begun at the age of 5. It was nice to visit the station in an official capacity instead of the earlier situation of being worried about the porter telling my friends and me that we would have to leave if we didn't behave ourselves. In those far off days of my youth the varity of locos at Headingley was amazing. 'A2s' and 'A3s' double-headed by 'D20s' or 'D49s' worked the Liverpool-Newcastle expresses, which are now four-car 158 'Express' units. 'G5s' worked the Ilkley trains and 'J21s' shunted the two separate goods yards - one was a flat yard and the other had the traditional NER coal drops.

A third siding was only used when the circus arrived in town. The first time this happened after the war we were allowed an afternoon off school to visit it. I was fortunate to see the animals being unloaded from the train at Headingley before their walk through the streets to Woodhouse Moor where the big top was erected.

25.8.64-26.8.64

Holmfirth This town is now immortalised in TV's 'Last of the Summer Wine', but in 1964 it was noteworthy merely for being at the end of a freight-only branch. My job for a couple of days was to operate the weighbridge and undertake the goods office work which was mainly received coal, as I recall.

28.8.64-5.9.64

Kippax This was a strange place on the single line from Garforth (on the Leeds-York line) to Castleford Old Station. Two of the sections of the line had conventional electric token working, but the third had the rather unusual directional lever system known locally as Transient Block. The lever referred to was a normal full-size signal lever and could only be pulled in the box at one end of the section at a time, provided the line was proved to be clear by an electrical system similar to a normal track circuit. The starting signal could then be cleared. There were a few coal trains from the delightfully named Primrose Hill colliery, worked by 'K1s' and 'Q6s'. Allerton Bywater Colliery, however, was inactive at the time as it was on strike. The station gardens at Kippax were well kept even though there was nobody to see them until 1968 when Prince Philip spent the night there in the Royal Train.

7.9.64-11.9.64

Trains Office A few days back in the Trains Office brought a sense of anticlimax to my period as a Station Master in the days of steam. My next SM job was to be at the end of 1967 when steam had virtually finished.

'O2' 2-8-0 No 63925, Misterton, 11.13 am, 28.4.62
This was not a very well-known location or line, situated between Gainsborough and Doncaster. However, there was quite a lot of activity there at the time. The loco betrays its GN origin but with a more modern cab; the pony-truck wheels look rather small, but otherwise the 'O2s' were fine-looking machines. It was a pity, though, that they were not usually kept clean. The first wagon is of rather curious construction and well loaded with scrap. Three Esso tanks make up part of the consist. Note that the point rodding in the foreground is of circular section.

'O2' 2-8-0 Nos 63931 and 63932, High Dyke, 3.41 pm, 18.7.62
If you were lucky, when travelling on the ECML south of Grantham, you might see some iron ore trains. This is a scene from history as there is now no home-produced ore in use. At High Dyke there was a steeply graded branch on the down side and the ore was taken from there to Scunthorpe. The locos were, of course, pure GN but with vacuum brakes to control the heavy loads. The wagons proclaim themselves to be tipplers, which means what it says, that they were tipped over sideways to unload rather than the inefficient and messy business of unloading by grab. Note the water crane near the brake van. The ECML is in the foreground, and in 1962 there were plenty of 'A4s' about.

'4F' 0-6-0 No 44315, Horbury Millfield Road, 11.4 am, 4.11.61, Down Class K
Locos working tender first had a special appeal to the photographer, but not, of course, to the men on the footplate. The driver is having to lean well out to observe the signals and it is a cold day, the full effects being suffered by both him and his fireman. There is a nice mixture of traffic. The leading brake van indicates a run-round and return to normal for the crew a little later. The loco is ex-works and carries the then new electrification warning signs on the tender. This reminded staff to beware of overhead wires when climbing on to the tender, changing lamps, etc. The gantry in the distance is remarkable as it has three distants but only one home signal.

'2MT' 2-6-0 No 46438, Horbury Millfield Road, 11.20 am, 4.11.61, 10.35 am Normanton-Sowerby Bridge parcels
This class of loco was much better adapted than most for tender-first running - it had a rather small coal bunker cut away to give a good view forward. I am not sure why there is a passenger brake next to the engine - perhaps it was due to a short-age of normal parcels vans. When the heavy mail order traffic from Bradford Exchange first started, the District Operating Superintendent turned out to see off the inaugural through train to King's Cross. He expressed his displeasure to us next morning - every single one of the ten 'parcels vans' had in fact been a non-corridor passenger coach with each compart-ment stuffed full of parcels!

The island platform at Millfield Road only served the middle two lines; note the platelayers hut, of a high standard with windows and a proper chimney.

'Q6' 0-8-0 No 63348, Leeds City, 1.9 pm, 8.3.61, Class J
This cross-Leeds transfer freight would have originated at Neville Hill and it is probably going to Hunslet. The line it is on goes round the back of the station, an area now with its own platform because of the increased passenger activity. My main memories of this end of the station are of the 'D20s' on the Selby locals. These fine NER 4-4-0s were reaching the end of their days in the 1950s; some District Office people used to go home for lunch at Cross Gates using the Selby trains. The departing Liverpool-Newcastle train has what later became known as a Class '40'; this was soon after diesels took over from 'Pacifics'.

'B1' 4-6-0 No 61129 and '4MT' 2-6-4T No 42410, Bradford Exchange, 8.34 am, 29.7.64
The old Bradford Exchange was, not surprisingly, very different from the newer Interchange. There were even gas lamps in use in 1964; note also that the platform number signs are suspended by long metal rods from the high roof and there are smoke deflectors attached to the screen at the entrance to the station. The two sides of the station - GN and L&Y - are illustrated here by the types of loco. It was always a busy parcels station as Bradford is the home of several mail order com-panies.

Semaphore signals were also still evident - two of them have white diamonds which indicated the presence of track cir-cuits and meant that the signalman would know if a train was standing at the signal; it was thus not necessary for a mem-ber of the train crew to go to the box, unless detained 'an unusually long time'. Bridge Street Goods Depot, in the back-ground, has also now disappeared, and the advertisement hoardings no doubt looked better from the other side.

'4F' 0-6-0 No 44044, Calverley and Rodley, 7.23 pm, 29.7.60, Down freight
'4Fs' were the workhorses of the LMS and tended to look rather ordinary, but I think, from this angle, they could appear quite attractive. It is always interesting, too, to see the driver and fireman carrying out their duties. They seem to be taking it easy in this shot as the train ambles along the Midland line which is pretty flat here in the Aire valley. The amount of trackwork is phenomenal for a wayside station. In the days of mechanical signalling, such a layout was expensive enough to install and maintain. When re-signalling took place and electric signals and points were brought into use, all such layouts had to be looked at very carefully due to the huge expense involved. Many are still being simplified - dequadrified (what an awful word!) or singled. On the up side are some articulated non-corridor coaches, stabled ready for future use. A fog hut and brick stove are provided between the fast and slow lines.

'WD' 2-8-0 No 90382, Maud's Bridge, 3.25 pm, 6.4.64, Up Class 8
I was never very keen on photographing 'WDs' - they were normally in a filthy condition and were not very attractive, in my view anyway. However, all railway photographers will appreciate the dilemma. You are a long way from home, there are not many trains about but there are some attractive lineside features. A train of some sort is needed to complete the picture and you have not much time to hang about waiting for the perfect loco.

This line was a successful GC venture into Lincolnshire with, of course, Immingham as the goal, as it still is. Nearby Scunthorpe also makes a considerable contribution. The GC box and signal are noteworthy, with the canal and old loading dock on the right. The trap points associated with the signal appear to be rather close to the main line. On the telegraph pole the telephone box is empty.

'K1' 2-6-0 No 62029, Bolton Percy, 4.4 pm, 8.8.64, Down Class 9
Today, not far from here the diverted ECML in its electrified glory runs in on the left. That was a long way into the future in 1964, when the four tracks were kept busy with Sheffield and Leeds traffic. This long mineral train, which includes a couple of vans, has been slotted in between holiday trains on a Saturday afternoon. The banner signal in front of the vans repeated a signal, some distance ahead, obscured by a bridge.

'Jubilee' 4-6-0 No 45573 *Newfoundland*, Armley Canal Road, 3.20 pm, 10.3.64, 3.25 pm Hunslet-Carlisle Canal Road was a rather grim station in a dreary part of Leeds, not helped by being down below the surrounding land; the two large island platforms were certainly more than adequate for the small number of passengers. This train continued to be hauled by a 'Jubilee' until almost the end of steam in the area in 1967. Of note are the car-carrying wagon next to the engine, and the lift tower above the left-hand end of the bridge; in the far distance a signal box is perched above the tracks.

'Princess Coronation' 4-6-2 No 46238 *City of Carlisle*, **Skipton, 2.20 pm, 27.9.63, North East Railtour**
I have never been a regular participant in railtours but there were, and still are, many that are well worth travelling on or observing from the lineside. This partic-ular tour lasted for a few days and is seen leaving Skipton for the Settle & Carlisle route. Skipton was a busy freight area and had an active loco shed. Beyond the 'Pacific' is a wagon repair siding, of which there were countless in those days. The building next to the signal box is of a similar design but at ground level. The guard of the passing freight train looks with interest at the tour loco which was a change from the usual 'Scots' and 'Jubilees'.

10
Conclusion
September 1964

To bring to a conclusion this personal view of the railways between 1954 and 1964 I must tell you that I, at last, became a Trainee in September 1964. Rather late in the day perhaps, but I waited until I had accumulated some experience of down to earth railway work before entering the very competitive exams and interviews for Management Training. It was a wonderful chance to have a good look at all the departments - Engineers, Telecoms and Loco depots, as well as the Commercial and Operating world with which I was familiar. I made sure of a fair amount of footplate experience, of course, but it was all diesel. This was a pity, but I made the point that it was necessary to see things from the train crew's point of view, and it was great fun in any case. My training took me all over the NE Region just before it ceased to exist in 1966.

Let us look at the things I learned about the duties of a Station Master and Goods Agent during my 22 months as a Trainee. An SM had, at all times, to have safety of the line as his main responsibility. The visits to signal boxes and level crossings were part of this. During these visits he also delivered vast amounts of paperwork, mainly STNs (Special Traffic Notices) and details of engineering work. The STNs showed extra trains, changes to existing ones, etc, which the signalman needed to know about when deciding on margins between trains, priority at junctions and other such matters. True, the trains shown were all carefully timed to fit in with the existing services, but things do not always go according to plan!

An old SM I knew, at Pontefract, recounted a tale about his signal box visits in the Malton area before the war. He made some of his visits by velocipede - little four-wheel trucks which ran along the line propelled by a large handle that you pushed up and down - these are often seen in silent films. Well, one signalman who had a bit of a grudge against him would send him through the section

with a bare margin ahead of the next train!

This SM also had a coal sale business, as many NER Station Masters had in addition to their normal jobs. It was quite legal and was, in fact, encouraged by the Management because the SM brought in more traffic by rail in order to boost his earnings. It appears to have been an NE practice and has now disappeared.

Out-of-hours visits to signal boxes were mandatory. You were supposed to visit each, once a month, outside normal office hours. After all, most boxes were open 24 hours a day and, if the signalmen knew they would only see you between 9 and 5, the odd rogue amongst them could get away with having unauthorised visitors or going to sleep, etc. On these occasions you carried out the normal checks but with special emphasis on night-time problems. Obviously the oil-lit signals came into this category and you would check to see that they showed a good light.

I had a trip from Newcastle to Carlisle on an evening signal sighting train and it was interesting to see the problems. One in particular was the half/half situation where the light was, maybe, quite bright but the arm did not rise high enough. The result was a part red, part green indication so far as the driver was concerned. No doubt it had been reported by a driver already, like so many other reports such as bumps in tunnels; a good local manager takes these matters seriously and gets something done. It is all part of the safety of the line and, of course, the passengers.

An autumn job was to check the fogmen in their duties and their knowledge of the Rules. These were platelayers who would be called out to place a detonator on the line at a distant signal and show a yellow flag or light to the driver if the signal was 'on'. If 'off' he would remove the detonator and show a green flag. It might be so foggy that he would have to climb part way up a tall signal to check its indication. One regular trick was to hang a bucket on the balancing arm near the base of the signal, so he would hear the change from 'on' to 'off'.

On the subject of detonators, there are a couple of incidents I remember which may be of interest. When I was Assistant Goods Agent at Dewsbury, one or two old, outdated 'dets' were discovered and there was a great debate as to how we could safely pack them and send them back to the manufacturers. I said I would sort out this problem. A long train of empties was about to depart so I put the dets on the rail about half way along the train, well away from driver and guard, and enjoyed the resulting harmless explosions. Well, I suppose there is a bit of the schoolboy Guy Fawkes in all of us!

On a similar matter, when SM at Castleford I was quite strongly recommended, by a signalman, to remove a detonator previously placed for legitimate reasons about 2 miles down the line, now the emergency was over. The signalman was quite right to point out that an exploding detonator always gives a driver an unpleasant shock, and I was out of order in leaving it there when there was no longer any reason.

In attending the aftermath of derailments I learned about a local manager's duties in this respect to add to my previous experiences, and it turned out to be very useful later when I was involved in countless such incidents. These were spread out over a period of many years, I hasten to add! Normally an SM was 'on call' alternate weeks and would be the first to be called to a mishap, where he had to decide what immediate action was required. My experiences very rarely involved passengers, who would obviously have priority. In freight derailments the first question was - do we need the steam crane? If so, that had to be ordered immediately as it would take some time to arrive. The breakdown crew were the normal fitters on duty at the local shed and they had to leave their work, sometimes for quite minor derailments. It might be necessary to remarshal the breakdown train before going down a single-line colliery branch, maybe with the crane leading to reach an awkward spot.

Next the Permanent Way Inspector and Signal & Telegraph technicians would probably be called out to deal with track and signal damage. I have a friend who was a Carriage & Wagon Foreman, and he would often be sent for if there was wagon damage. He was pretty liberal with his red and green labels which were put in the wagon label clip to denote 'crippled'. It is a serious offence, of course, if any unauthorised person removes one of these labels. He once put a red card on my car to tell me that a tyre was flat! On another occasion, after a large pile-up at Royston, he climbed 30 feet up an embankment to put a card on a wheel-less 21-ton hopper, placed out

of the way by the steam crane. Another of his regular problems was that certain collieries misused BR wagons within the precincts by turning them over on the tippler. This resulted in loss of oil from the axle boxes and subsequent smoking 'hot boxes' out on the main line. I once saw a train with three of these passing Streethouse.

Rerailing and clearing up the debris was the next job at any mishap, then the inevitable paperwork was necessary. The main point was to find the cause, and make sure it did not happen again. This was not easy as the Engineer would say that it was not his track that was to blame. On one occasion I pointed out that, on one 60-foot length of track, half the keys (which secured the the rail to the chair on the sleeper) were missing - probably they were being used as firewood by the locals. The ganger had to admit that the loco was sitting on the ballast due to a slight case of 'road spread'.

One incident in the Pontefract area involved the Rowntrees chocolate train - several wagons became derailed and turned over. It was a hot day and there was melted chocolate all over the place. A friend of mine was in charge and it was pointed out to him that the work would proceed faster if some liquid refreshment could be fetched from the local pub. Unfortunately the only containers available to convey the large quantities needed were ones which had previously held liquid soap. The results were frothy to say the least!

There was quite a lot of steam around in the North East. In particular the Mineral Leading jobs on Tyneside still employed quite large numbers of 'J27s' and 'Q6s'. I found the area near King Edward bridge rewarding from a photographic point of view and it was also interesting to see the juxtaposition of steam and third rail electrification on Tyneside. Both have now gone, of course.

The days of steam were drawing to a close and it was, perhaps, appropriate to be in the North East at this time, where it all began. It lingered on in some places for a little while longer but, by the time I returned to an SM job, there was very little left anywhere. It was a privilege and pleasure to work with steam for ten years in a variety of jobs, some more acceptable than others. I count myself fortunate to have been around when steam was a normal day-to-day feature, and can understand those who arrived on the scene a little late and had to race around to catch the last few wisps. However, all is not lost. There is still plenty of interest for those who work on the railways as well as for those to whom it is a fascinating hobby and maybe even, as I said at the beginning, a whole way of life.

'OF' 0-4-0ST No 51244, Goole Docks, 2.31 pm, 8.10.60

It is almost beyond belief that such a loco was in daily use 30 years ago and at a location with heavy amounts of traffic. The obvious question is - where was the coal kept? The rather capacious cab appears to be the answer. Note the enclosed piston rod, the collection of oil cans above it, and the block buffers. The old lady was nearly 70 years old at the time.

The BD container on the right, and the smaller A type, were very popular for many years. They were used for Ministry of Defence traffic, car tyres, household removals and many other jobs. Target '29' is displayed on the loco front and back so that nobody could be in doubt as to which diagram it was working.

The word 'diagram' is used a great deal in railway circles and often causes confusion to other people. Railways have more than their fair share of such jargon, although no more so than, say, the computer world or others which have accumulated buzz words in a much shorter time-span. Diagram means, merely, the printed set of timings to which a trip engine, etc, works. It will show the time off shed, movement to start point of work, and the other movements during the shift. Associated with it will be the men's diagrams - what time they sign on and off - as well as the details of their planned work.

'A3' 4-6-2 No 60040 *Cameronian*, Darlington, 4.34 pm, 29.5.60

It was a pity that this fine loco was only on standby duty, although it was quite common, at one time, to have such provision in case of main-line failures. You could also usually see an 'A1' or other 'Pacific' in steam at Doncaster ready for action. Note the 'banjo' dome, so called because when viewed from above it assumed the shape of that instrument. The loco also has fine lining out and an early BR totem on the tender. Apart from the station, Darlington is only a shadow of its former self, the loco shed and Works now having closed.

'A1' 4-6-2 No 60142 *Edward Fletcher* and 'A3' 4-6-2 No 60040 *Cameronian*, Tweedmouth Shed, 6.7 pm, 17.4.64

Tweedmouth was always an active place, but it was difficult to see how a shed of that size could survive for so long. The fact that there are three 'Pacifics' in view with two in steam is also notable. In the early days of diesels there were many cases of steam substitution for failed diesels on both passenger and long-distance freight. Possibly this was the reason for the survival of the shed and these lovely locos when, in the harsh world of the accountants, they should have gone to the breakers. In the mid-'50s you could still see North British engines here.

As an employee of the NE Region I was able to use a local free pass to travel from Leeds to Berwick, so I came to know the locality well - you only received one pass per year outside your own Region. A summer Saturday spent at Tweedmouth or at the Berwick end of the Royal Border Bridge was well worthwhile; the Haymarket 'Pacifics' tended not to be seen south of Newcastle but came through Berwick in abundance. I saw my last 'A3' there - No 60087 *Blenheim* - and my wife uses 'Trimbush' as a kennel name; that was another favourite loco in the area.

'J94' 0-6-0ST Nos 68015/25/45/39/37, Darlington Shed, 4.25 pm, 29.5.60
Not one of my favourite classes, but the symmetry of the photo appeals to me; the unsightly pipework below the cab spoiled the appearance of a locos, which was somewhat utilitarian in aspect in any case, but they performed a wide variety of shunting jobs in the Darlington area.

The shed served a busy passenger and freight locality and, in addition, was always packed with locos waiting to go into or just coming out of the famous Works. There was always plenty to see, particularly of an NE origin. However, when I was very young the Works were notable for dealing with 'Sandringhams' which then ran in on Leeds trains - *Champion Lodge* was one I particularly remember.

'J72' 0-6-0T No 68684, Thornaby Shed, 4.0 pm, 19.7.59
A visit to Thornaby in 1959 revealed that the large loco shed had been rebuilt, which seemed rather strange so near the end of steam. However, Teesside was, as now, an extremely busy freight area and it was no doubt considered worthwhile, to keep things going. It was later adapted for diesel use and continues to be a busy shed to this day. Of note is the practice of marshalling locos of a particular class together. Other types, such as 'Q6' and 'J27', were similarly segregated. These 'J72' tanks were used on the docks, in goods depots and yards. The adjacent Tees Yard is still operating, but not in its old form of using hump and flat shunting methods.

'Q6' 0-8-0 No 63353, Durham, 1.7 pm, 27.9.61, Up Class J
I have included this to show how signals, left to their own devices, can proliferate. Could any more have been crammed into such a small space? The 'Q6' is entering Durham from the north with a heavy train of 21-ton hoppers, very common in that part of the world for so long, but now no more. Note the absence of a vacuum pipe on the loco, and the rather pleasing double-sided platform seat. The classical dimensions of the base of the lamp post are spoiled by the bare bulbs and wires going from one lamp to the next.

'K1' 2-6-0 No 62045, Northallerton, 12.32 pm, 4.2.61, Down Class H
It is a cold February day in the North East, and the freight is presumably heading for Darlington as it is not using the dive-under for Stockton. The station, with staggered platforms, has now changed a lot – the roof has gone and there are fewer platforms since the Leeds via Ripon service disappeared.

It was close to this spot that one of the greatest near misses of all time took place. The story is well known and involved an express coming off the Ripon line and another, on the main line, which was over-running signals at danger. The Ripon driver, although he 'had the road' with all signals 'off', saw what was happening and stopped in time. Relief for all concerned!

Northallerton was also, at one time, the junction for the Wensleydale service, and it is nice to know that there are still freight trains on that line, for the time being at least.

'2MT' 2-6-0 No 46476, Alnmouth, 1.7 pm, 25.11.61, 1.10 pm to Alnwick

I was lucky to get this photo, taken from the window of a train. My train was the 10.0 am York-Edinburgh with six coaches in the charge of 'A3' 4-6-2 No 60082 *Neil Gow*. I was travelling to Dunbar in order to get to Burnmouth for a visit to the threatened Eyemouth branch. It was the only way to get there but, as it was 3.30 pm when I reached Burnmouth and less than a month from the winter solstice, the chances of getting good photos were remote.

Photos taken from a train depend for their success on where you are when the train stops, or whether you have time to jump out and run down the platform without risking your continued journey. I do not remember the Ivatt Class '2s' being very common on the Alnwick branch. The shed stands on the right; it and the branch had about 5 years left. Note the station seat, complete with snakes, and parked rather near the platform edge. Alnmouth station is still with us on the newly electrified ECML, and the line hereabouts offers one of the highlights of the journey where you can look across the estuary to the village - lovely on a summer evening.

'J27' 0-6-0 No 65815, Heaton, 3.28 pm, 10.6.65
Steam is nearly at an end but in the home of Geordie Stephenson there is still much activity. This is a curious juxtaposition of steam and electric railway. The third rail system only had a few more years to run before replacement by diesel and then, eventually, by the innovative and successful Tyneside Metro System which showed that Geordie inventiveness still lived. The footpath for railway staff on the left illustrates the best in safety practice - you go round the water tank and back up the hill, not across the railway. The J27 is on a typical Mineral Leading job (surely a Tyneside term) - the 21-ton hoppers are probably on the way to shipping staithes. On the right are Heaton Carriage Sidings and shed.

A cavalcade of Pullmans

'A3' 4-6-2 No 60036 *Colombo*, Headingley, 4.17 pm, 27.5.61, Up 'Queen of Scots Pullman'

This was the location where I first saw the Queen of Scots when it started running after the war. Colombo was a regular loco on this train for many years, north of Leeds, and is carrying a spare headboard, reversed, on the bufferbeam. A North Eastern slotted post signal is the down starter next to the signal box and level crossing in the distance. The siding on the left served the coal drops, while that on the right was only used, so far as I remember, for the circus train. There are just the two lines here now, and even the level crossing has

disappeared along with the NER box. 'Pacers', including the rather odd Class '141s', provide a frequent service at Headingley, home of Yorkshire cricket and scene of many a stirring Test match; you can now travel at almost any hour of the day, including Sundays.

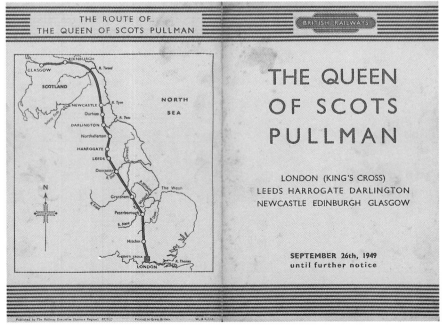

THE ROUTE OF
THE QUEEN OF SCOTS PULLMAN

BRITISH RAILWAYS

THE QUEEN
OF SCOTS
PULLMAN

LONDON (KING'S CROSS)
LEEDS HARROGATE DARLINGTON
NEWCASTLE EDINBURGH GLASGOW

SEPTEMBER 26th, 1949
until further notice

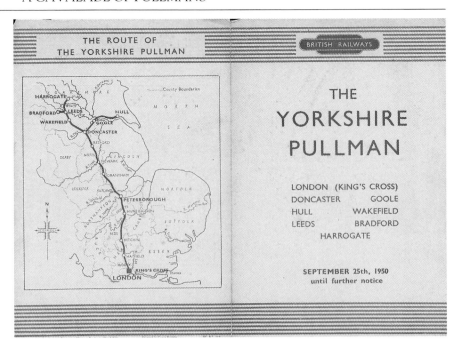

'A2/3' 4-6-2 No 60519 *Honeyway*, Leeds Central, 3.47 pm, 12.8.61
The 'Queen of Scots' was one of the premier trains of the day at Leeds Central, but I was not bothering with it in 1961 as it had gone over to Class '40' haulage. How things have changed - years later people would have travelled many miles to photograph such a combination! *Honeyway* was a very rare visitor to Leeds. She had worked into Leeds on the 10.52 am King's Cross to Ripon. Why a Haymarket 'A2/3' should power such a train is a mystery. Her train was worked forward to Ripon by Standard 2-6-4T No 80116.

'A1' 4-6-2 No 60121 *Silurian*, Holbeck, 4.41 pm, 25.4.62, Up 'Queen of Scots Pullman'
A fine-sounding loco on a fine train, *Silurian* is using the spur from the Harrogate line to reach the high level adjacent to Holbeck station; the low-level platform and subway can be seen at the extreme left. Behind the loco is the Leeds & Thirsk Railway engine roundhouse. The through route which enabled the train to travel from Glasgow via Harrogate has now gone, and so has the train.

'A3' 4-6-2 No 60039 *Sandwich*, Ardsley, 8.57 pm, 28.6.61, Down 'Yorkshire Pullman'
It was always an ambition of mine to catch the down Pullman at the northern end of its journey, but it arrived in Leeds so late in the evening that midsummer was the only occasion when this was possible - the low light shows up the clean lines of the 'A3' to advantage. As was often the case, the Pullman brake is of an older vintage than the remainder of the train. Note the rather dreadful wooden buildings on the right beneath an old slagheap.

'V1' 2-6-2T No 67640, Goole, 11.0 am, 7.11.61, Up 'Yorkshire Pullman'
I sometimes wonder why I bothered taking photos in winter, particularly in the fog! However, this was the only time I had chance to record the Hull portion of the Pullman and I did not see many Class 'V1s' round that area either. I suppose, looking back now to a period telescoped and crystallised in time and with many other things to do, I was fortunate to cover as much as I did. Goole, known to a few as 'Sleepy Hollow', sometimes suffers from damage to the Ouse bridge caused by barges, and threats to the Hull-Doncaster services via that route as a result. Note the grim wooden platforms, two-wheel barrow and LNER-style lamps. On the right, amidst the gloom, is a fully-fledged loading gauge in the goods yard. In the days when large, bulky loads were regularly carried, the wagons would be pushed under this gauge by the pilot to see whether the load was within the maximum profile as regards height and width. Nowadays, Goole has a frequent service of 'Sprinters' and the docks continue to be busy.

'Black Five' 4-6-0 No 45207, Bramley, Leeds, 10.26 am, 2.6.60, Bradford portion of the Up 'Yorkshire Pullman'
This was the premier train of the day at Bramley, even though it did not call there. Note the non-Pullman coach next to the loco; this was intended to provide a service for local passengers between Bradford and Leeds who did not wish to pay the supplementary fare - there were some thrifty people in those parts! The coach returned in the evening on the down Pullman and again helped to fill in a gap in the local service. Imagine the amount of shunting this involved in attaching the coach as well as the splitting of the various portions at Leeds Central. The coach also had a brake compartment and this meant that a Pullman brake was unnecessary, but the Harrogate and Hull portions both had them.

For a few glorious weeks in 1961 a genuine Great Western coach, by some fluke, found its way on to this job. My colleagues on Distribution of Coaching Stock tried to keep this going but higher authority was adamant - it was Out of Gauge and must be returned to the Broad Gauge railway immediately! Eventually it did so, by freight train complete with out-of-gauge bell signals from box to box.

Note the GN somersault signals and 'J39' pilot using a long line of barrier wagons to place a wagon in Turner's siding.

'A1' 4-6-2 No 60126 *Sir Vincent Raven*, Normanton, 2.35 pm, 14.1.62, Down 'Harrogate Sunday Pullman'
This was one of the lesser-known Pullmans and Normanton was not, of course, on its normal route. It was passing this way due to a normal Sunday hazard - engineering work - which made this particular train one of the more adventurous on which to travel. The Pullman brake in the middle of the train shows that the train will be split at Leeds into Bradford and Harrogate portions. Nowadays this is the termination of the northern end of the Midland main line, there being a gap from Goose Hill to Wath Road, near Rotherham. This situation flies in the face of the commonly held view that the early routes, promoted by people like the infamous George Hudson, were the ones to survive. Certainly Hudson was very active in the Normanton area.

There are several 'dollies' in the picture, each having a white repeater bar at the back to serve as a warning to staff on the line that a loco or train is due. The fair-sized engine shed on the left provided mainly freight locos, including the 'WD' just about to leave. Note the large coaling plant which didn't have to look far for its supplies of coal; the plant, like the shed, has disappeared.

Tailpiece: Howden Clough, 4.27 pm, 22.7.61, 1.30 pm (SO) Cleethorpes-Bradford Exchange
The train is passing the switched-out box on the steeply-graded GN Dewsbury branch. There were very few ex-GN somersault signals of this type left, that is those with the spectacles part way down the post. No doubt it was retained because the box was little used; it was only switched in occasionally when the local sidings needed to be served. Even on a summer Saturday, when there were many extra trains about, it remained closed.
    Note the LNER stock with the buckeye coupling in the down, out of use, position. At this time there was still plenty of screw-coupled stock in use, but the overwhelming safety advantages of the buckeye prevailed, and it is now universal.

Index